SECURITIES LAW:
INSIDER TRADING

by

STEPHEN M. BAINBRIDGE
Professor, UCLA School of Law

TURNING POINT SERIES®

New York
Foundation

D1248583

Cover Drawing: John MacDonald
Williamstown, Massachusetts
Cover Design: Keith Stout
Manhattan, New York

Turning Point Series is a registered trademark
used herein under license.

COPYRIGHT © 1999 By FOUNDATION PRESS
11 Penn Plaza, Tenth Floor
New York, NY 10001
Phone (212) 760–8700
Fax (212) 760–8705

Printed in the United States of America

ISBN 1–56662–737–0

 TEXT IS PRINTED ON 10% POST
CONSUMER RECYCLED PAPER

TURNING POINT SERIES

- **CIVIL PROCEDURE: TERRITORIAL JURISDICTION AND VENUE**
  Kevin M. Clermont, Cornell University
- **CIVIL PROCEDURE: CLASS ACTIONS**
  Linda S. Mullenix, University of Texas (Available August 1999)
- **CONSTITUTIONAL LAW: EQUAL PROTECTION**
  Louis Michael Seidman, Georgetown (Available August 2002)
- **SECURITIES LAW: INSIDER TRADING**
  Stephen M. Bainbridge, UCLA
- **STATUTORY INTERPRETATION**
  Kent R. Greenawalt, Columbia University (Available July1999)
- **TORT LAW: PROXIMATE CAUSE**
  Joseph A. Page, Georgetown (Available August 2000)

*

About the Author

BAINBRIDGE, STEPHEN; Professor of Law, University of California, Los Angeles. Formerly a professor at the University of Illinois College of Law and a visiting professor at UCLA in '96–97, he joined the UCLA faculty in fall 1997. He teaches Business Associations, Corporate Finance, Securities Regulation, and Mergers and Acquisitions. He attended the University of Virginia School of Law, and, after law school, Bainbridge clerked for the late Frank A. Kaufman, who was then the Chief Judge of the U.S. District Court for the District of Maryland. He then worked for several years as an associate with the law firm of Arnold & Porter in Washington, D.C. before becoming a professor. He has written numerous law review articles on a variety of subjects, but with a strong emphasis on the law and economics of public corporations. His recent publications include: The 1999 Supplement (with Teacher's Manual) to "Cases and Materials on Business Associations: Agency Partnerships and Corporations" (Foundation Press 3d ed. 1998), which he co-wrote with William A. Klein and J. Mark Ramseyer; "Community and Statism: A Conservative Contractarian Critique of Progressive Corporate Law Scholarship," 82 Cornell Law Review 856 (1997); "Participatory Management Within a Theory of the Firm," 21

Journal of Corporation Law 657 (1996); "Securities Act Section 12(2) After the Gustafson Debacle," 50 Business Lawyer 1231 (1995); "Incorporating State Law Fiduciary Duties Into the Federal Insider Trading Prohibition," 52 Washington and Lee Law Review 1189 (1995).

Table of Contents

SECURITIES LAW:

INSIDER TRADING

*

CHAPTER 1

INTRODUCTION

The term insider trading is something of a misnomer. It conjures up images of corporate directors or officers using secret information to buy stock from (or sell it to) unsuspecting investors. To be sure, the modern federal insider trading prohibition proscribes a corporation's officers and directors from trading on the basis of material nonpublic information about their firm, but it also casts a far broader net. Consider the following people who have been convicted of illegal insider trading in recent years:

- A partner in a law firm representing the acquiring company in a hostile takeover bid who traded in target company stock.

- A Wall Street Journal columnist who traded prior to publication of his column in the stock of companies he wrote about.

- A psychiatrist who traded on the basis of information learned from a patient.

- A financial printer who traded in the stock of companies about which he was preparing disclosure documents.

As you can see, the phrase insider trading thus includes a wide range of individuals who trade in a

1

corporation's stock on the basis of material information unknown by the investing public at large.

Insider trading is covered by a number of legal regimes, of which no less than 5 are important for our purposes:

- The disclose or abstain rule under § 10(b) of the Securities Exchange Act of 1934 and Securities and Exchange Commission Rule 10b–5 thereunder, which is principally concerned with classic insiders such as corporate officers and directors;[1]

- The misappropriation theory under § 10(b) and Rule 10b–5, which deals mainly with persons outside the company in whose stock they traded;

- SEC Rule 14e–3 under Exchange Act § 14(e), which is limited to insider trading in connection with a tender offer;

- Section 16(b) of the Exchange Act, which prohibits corporate directors, officers, and shareholders owning more than 10% of the firm's stock from earning "short swing profits" by buying and selling stock in a six month period;

- State corporate law, which principally targets corporate officers and directors who buy stock from shareholders of their company in face-to-face transactions.

All five regulatory schemes are discussed in the chapters that follow, but our attention will focus

1. The Securities and Exchange Commission (Commission or SEC) is an independent agency created by Congress in the

mainly on the federal prohibition under SEC Rule 10b–5.

At the beginning of the 1900s, state corporate law was the only legal regime regulating insider trading. At that time, as is still true in some states, corporate law allowed insider trading. The state common law of insider trading, however, has been largely superseded by federal securities law, especially Rule 10b–5. To be sure, the state rules are still on the books and are still used in a few cases that fall through the cracks of the federal regulatory scheme, but federal law offers regulators and plaintiffs so many procedural and substantive advantages that it has become the dominant legal regime in this area. The most important feature of federal law, however, may be that it put a cop on the beat. State law relied on firms and shareholders to detect and prosecute insider trading. Under federal law, the SEC and the Justice Department can prosecute inside traders, which has substantially increased the likelihood it will be detected and successfully prosecuted.

A truly significant distinguishing feature of the federal insider trading prohibition has been change.

Securities Exchange Act to enforce the various federal securities laws. Congress gave the SEC power to supplement the securities statutes with various rules and regulations, among which are rules 10b–5 and 14e–3 governing insider trading. Congress also gave the SEC power to investigate alleged violations of the securities laws and to bring civil actions against suspected violators. Most insider trading actions are handled by the SEC's Division of Enforcement, which is the litigation arm of the SEC.

Although the prohibition is only about three decades old, it has seen more shifts in doctrine than most corporate law rules have seen in the last century. Exploring this rich history is a useful exercise—in many respects you cannot understand today's issues without the historical background—but is also is fraught with danger: you must draw clear distinctions between what *was* the law and what *is* the law.

One point requiring particular attention is the evolution of new theories on which insider trading liability can be based. We shall see two very important cases in which the Supreme Court restricted the scope of the traditional disclose or abstain rule. In response to those cases, the SEC and the lower courts developed two new theories on which liability could be imposed. As we move through this material, pay close attention to which theory is being discussed at any given moment and consider how that theory differs from the others.

The Policy Debate

Insider trading is one of the most common violations of the federal securities laws. It is certainly the violation that has most clearly captured the public's imagination—indeed, what other corporate or securities law doctrine provided the plot line of a major motion picture, as insider trading did in Oliver Stone's *Wall Street* (1987)? But insider trading also remains one of the most controversial aspects of securities law. Courts and regulators typically justify the prohibition on fairness or other equity grounds. Is insider trading clearly unfair, however? People who trade with an insider who has access to nonpublic information probably feel they were cheated. According to one poll, however, well over half of all Americans would trade on inside information if given the chance. Whether insider trading is unfair thus depends on the eye of the beholder.

Many leading corporate law scholars contend that the legality of insider trading should turn not on fairness considerations, but rather on issues of economic efficiency. Some of these commentators believe that the prohibition cannot be justified on efficiency grounds, while others have offered various economic justifications for the prohibition.

Although virtually no one seriously believes that the federal insider trading prohibition is likely to be repealed any time soon, the academic policy debate nevertheless rewards study. Understanding the policy issues at stake can help inform the way in which unresolved aspects of the prohibition are settled. For law students, a review of the policy debate also has considerable instrumental value. The insider trading debate cannot be understood without considering the so-called "law and economics" school of jurisprudence. Many corporate law teachers are practitioners of law and economics, while even those who are not often feel compelled to introduce their students to this mode of legal reasoning. Insider trading is one of the widely-used vehicles for introducing law and economics to corporate law students. Accordingly, we shall devote some attention to developing the economic tools necessary to understanding the debate, as well as the policy debate itself.

CHAPTER 2

ORIGINS OF THE INSIDER TRADING PROHIBITION

Although we now take it for granted that regulating insider trading is a job for the SEC under federal law, it was not always so. Until quite recently, insider trading was handled as a matter of state corporate law. To be sure, the federal prohibition has largely eclipsed state law in this area, but the older state rules are still worth studying. The historical evolution of the insider trading prohibition is not only relevant to understanding current doctrine, but also is highly relevant to understanding the on-going policy debate over the merits of insider trading regulation. This chapter therefore begins with a review of the state common law of insider trading. It then turns to the statutory origins of the federal prohibition, such as they are, leaving the judicial development of current federal doctrine for the next chapter.

The State Common Law of Insider Trading

Our overview of the state common law of insider trading is both historical and functional. We'll look first at the three different insider trading rules states adopted in the early 1900s. It turns out that these rules were largely limited to face-to-face

7

transactions, however, so we will then look at how states regulated insider trading in the context of stock market transactions. Completing those two tasks will carry us through the 1930s, when the federal securities laws were adopted, but we'll defer development of federal law in order to look at how state corporate law treats insider trading today.

Three Rules for Face–to–Face Transactions

Prior to 1900 it was treatise law that "[t]he doctrine that officers and directors [of corporations] are trustees of the stockholders ... does not extend to their private dealings with stockholders or others, though in such dealings they take advantage of knowledge gained through their official position."[2] Under this so-called "majority" or "no duty" rule, liability was based solely on actual fraud, such as misrepresentation or fraudulent concealment of a material fact. As one court explained, liability arose only where the defendant said or did something "to divert or prevent, and which did divert or prevent, the plaintiff from looking into, or making inquiry, or further inquiries, as to the affairs or condition of the company and its prospects for dividends...."[3]

The first tentative step towards the modern prohibition came in *Oliver v. Oliver,*[4] in which the

2. H. L. Wilgus, *Purchase of Shares of a Corporation by a Director from a Shareholder*, 8 Mich. L. Rev. 267 (1910).

3. *Carpenter v. Danforth*, 52 Barb. 581, 589 (N.Y.Sup.Ct. 1868).

4. 45 S.E. 232 (Ga. 1903).

Georgia Supreme Court announced the so-called "minority" or "duty to disclose" rule. Under *Oliver*, directors who obtained inside information by virtue of their position held the information in trust for the shareholders. Accordingly, directors had a duty to disclose all material information to shareholders before trading with them.

In *Strong v. Repide*,[5] the U.S. Supreme Court offered a third approach to the insider trading problem. The court acknowledged the majority rule, but declined to follow it. Instead, the court held that, under the particular factual circumstances of the case at bar, "the law would indeed be impotent if the sale could not be set aside or the defendant cast in damages for his fraud." Thus was born the so-called "special facts" or "special circumstances" rule, which holds that although directors generally owe no duty to disclose material facts when trading with shareholders, such a duty can arise in—as the name suggests—"special circumstances." What facts were sufficiently "special" for a court to invoke the rule? *Strong v. Repide* identified the two most important fact patterns: Concealment of identity by the defendant and failure to disclose significant facts having a dramatic impact on the stock price.

As state law evolved in the early 1900s, both the special circumstances and minority rules rapidly gained adherents.[6] Every court faced with the issue

5. 213 U.S. 419 (1909).

6. Given that both the special circumstances and minority rules were based on the director or officer's fiduciary duties, a

during this period felt obliged to discuss all three rules. While many courts adhered to the majority rule, they typically went out of their way to demonstrate that the case at bar in fact did not involve any special facts. Even more strikingly, during this period no court deciding the issue as a matter of first impression adopted the old majority rule. As a result, by the late 1930s, a headcount of cases indicated that the special circumstances rule prevailed in a plurality of states, the older no duty rule no longer commanded a majority, and the duty to disclose rule had been adopted in a substantial number—albeit, still a minority—of states.[7]

problem arose: What happened when a director sold shares, rather than buying them? A director who buys shares is trading with someone who is already a shareholder of the corporation and, as such, someone to whom the director has fiduciary obligations. A director who sells shares, however, likely is dealing with a stranger, someone not yet a shareholder and, as such, not yet someone to whom the director owes any duties. Assuming *arguendo* that the director's fiduciary duties to shareholders proscribe buying shares from them on the basis of undisclosed material information, the logic of that rule does not necessarily extend to cases in which the director sells to an outsider. As with most questions of state law in this area, the issue is not solely of historical or academic interest. As we shall see, the modern federal insider trading prohibition is also premised on a violation of fiduciary duty. Unfortunately, while the federal prohibition indisputably applies both to insiders who buy and those who sell, state law remains uncertain. Most academic commentators believe state law applied only to those insiders who buy existing shareholders, but relevant precedents are rare and consist mostly of dictum.

7. I. Beverly Lake, *The Use for Personal Profit of Knowledge Gained While a Director*, 9 Miss. L.J. 427,448–49 (1937).

Stock Market Transactions

Both the special circumstances and minority rules were more limited in scope than may appear at first blush. Most of the cases in which plaintiffs succeeded involved some form of active fraud, not just a failure to disclose. More important, all of these cases involved face-to-face transactions. The vast majority of stock transactions, both then and now, take place on impersonal stock exchanges. In order to be economically significant, an insider trading prohibition must apply to such transactions as well as face-to-face ones.

The leading state case in this area, still found in most corporations casebooks, is *Goodwin v. Agassiz*.[8] Ignoring some factual complexities unnecessary to understanding the opinion, what happened here is a classic insider trading story: Defendants were directors and senior officers of a mining corporation. A geologist working for the company advanced a theory suggesting there might be substantial copper deposits in northern Michigan. The company thought the theory had merit and began securing mineral rights on the relevant tracts of land. Meanwhile, the defendants began buying shares on the market. Plaintiff was a former stockholder who had sold his shares on the stock market. The defendants apparently had bought the shares, although neither side knew the identity of the other party to the transaction until much later. When the true facts became known, plaintiff sued the directors, arguing that he would not have sold if the geologist's theory

8.   186 N.E. 659 (Mass.1933).

had been disclosed. The court rejected plaintiff's claim, concluding that defendants had no duty to disclose the theory before trading.

Goodwin is commonly read as standing for the proposition that directors and officers trading on an impersonal stock exchange owe no duty of disclosure to the persons with whom they trade. Although that reading is correct as a bottom line matter, it ignores some potentially important doctrinal complications. The Massachusetts Supreme Judicial court's analysis begins with a nod to the old majority rule, opining that directors generally do not "occupy the position of trustee toward individual stockholders in the corporation."[9] The court went on, however, to note that "circumstances may exist ... [such] that an equitable responsibility arises to communicate facts," which sounds like the special circumstances rule. Indeed, the court made clear that Massachusetts would apply the special circumstances rule to face-to-face transactions: "where a director personally seeks out a stockholder for the purpose of buying his shares without making disclosure of material facts within his peculiar knowledge and not within reach of the stockholder, the transaction will be closely scrutinized and relief may be granted in appropriate instances." Was the court likewise applying the special circumstances rule to stock market transactions? Perhaps. The court took pains to carefully analyze the nature of the information in question, concluding that it was "at most a hope," and was careful to say that there was no

9. *Goodwin*, 186 N.E. at 660.

affirmative duty to disclose under the circumstances at bar. At the same time, however, the dispositive special circumstance clearly was the stock market context. As to transactions effected on an impersonal exchange, no duty to disclose would be imposed.

Given that federal law later imposed just such a duty, it is instructive to carefully examine the court's explanation for its holding:

> Purchases and sales of stock dealt in on the stock exchange are commonly impersonal affairs. An honest director would be in a difficult situation if he could neither buy nor sell on the stock exchange shares of stock in his corporation without first seeking out the other actual ultimate party to the transaction and disclosing to him everything which a court or jury might later find that he then knew affecting the real or speculative value of such shares. Business of that nature is a matter to be governed by practical rules. Fiduciary obligations of directors ought not to be made so onerous that men of experience and ability will be deterred from accepting such office. Law in its sanctions is not coextensive with morality. It cannot undertake to put all parties to every contract on an equality as to knowledge, experience, skill and shrewdness. It cannot undertake to relieve against hard bargains made between competent parties without fraud.[10]

The insider trading prohibition's defenders find much that is contestable in the court's rationale.

10. Id.

Two observations suffice for present purposes: First, notice the strongly normative (and strongly laissez faire) tone of the quoted passage. Why can't the law undertake to ensure that all parties to stock market transaction have at least roughly equal access to information? This question turns out to be one of insider trading jurisprudence's recurring issues. Second, consider the "difficult situation" the court claims an insider trading prohibition would create for "honest directors." Even at its most expansive, the federal insider trading prohibition never required directors to individually seek out those with whom they trade and personally make disclosure of "everything" they know about the company. A workable insider trading prohibition simply requires directors to publicly disclose all material facts in their possession before trading or, if they are not able to do so, to refrain from trading. Corporate policies could be developed to limit director and officer trading to windows of time in which there is unlikely to be significant undisclosed information, such as those following dissemination of periodic corporate disclosures. An inconvenience for all concerned, to be sure, but hardly enough to keep able people from serving as directors of publicly traded corporations. Not surprisingly, this aspect of the court's rationale has gotten short shrift from later courts.

State Common Law Today

About the same time as *Goodwin* was being decided, the New Deal Congresses began adopting the federal securities laws. Although those laws did not preempt state corporate law, federal regulation has essentially superseded them insofar as insider trading is concerned. State law is not just a historical footnote, however. Some cases still fall though the federal cracks, being left for state law to decide. Plaintiffs still sometimes include a state law-based count in their complaints. Most important, we will see that state law ought to provide the basic analytical framework within which the federal regime operates. Having said that, however, it must be admitted that the ever-increasing focus of regulators and litigators on federal law aborted the evolution of state common law in this area. With one important exception, discussed below, we are still more or less where we were in the late 1930s.

Although both the special circumstances and minority rules continued to pick up adherents during the decades after *Goodwin* was decided,[11] a number of states continue to adhere to the no duty rule.[12] Insofar as stock market transactions are concerned,

11. See, e.g., *Broffe v. Horton*, 172 F.2d 489 (2d Cir.1949) (diversity case); *Childs v. RIC Group, Inc.*, 331 F.Supp. 1078, 1081 (N.D.Ga.1970), aff'd, 447 F.2d 1407 (5th Cir.1971) (diversity case); *Hobart v. Hobart Estate Co.*, 159 P.2d 958 (Cal.1945). An early line of federal cases arising under Rule 10b–5 applied the special circumstances and, more often, the fiduciary duty rules to face-to-face insider trading transactions. See, e.g., *Kohler v. Kohler Co.*, 319 F.2d 634 (7th Cir.1963); *Speed v. Transamerica Corp.*, 99 F.Supp. 808 (D.Del.1951).

12. See, e.g., *Goodman v. Poland*, 395 F.Supp. 660, 678–80 (D.Md. 1975); *Fleetwood Corp. v. Mirich*, 404 N.E.2d 38, 46 (Ind.App.1980); Yerke v. Batman, 376 N.E.2d 1211, 1214 (Ind. App.1978).

moreover, *Goodwin* apparently remains the prevailing view.[13] The leading cases are of considerable antiquity, however, so one can easily imagine lawyers arguing that the old no duty precedents should not be followed today. As they might point out, the American Law Institute's Principles of Corporate Governance (a scaled-down version of the ALI's famous Restatements) opine that a duty to disclose exists in both face-to-face and stock market transactions,[14] albeit as yet without much case law support.

Derivative Liability for Insider Trading Under State Corporate Law

Although the Massachusetts court in *Goodwin* rejected the argument that directors "occupy the position of trustee towards individual stockholders,"[15] it also recognized that directors are fiduciaries of the corporate enterprise. Its holdings barring shareholders from seeking direct relief thus did not prohibit corporate actions against insider traders. Although a leading case did not emerge until the 1960s, litigators eventually stumbled on the possibility of derivative litigation against inside traders.

All of the cases we have been discussing thus far were brought as direct actions; i.e., cases in which the plaintiff shareholder sued in his own name seeking compensation for the injury done to him by

13.   3A Fletcher Cyc Corp ¶ 1168.1 (Perm. Ed. 1986).

14.   American Law Institute, Principles of Corporate Governance: Analysis and Recommendations § 5.04 (1992).

15.   *Goodwin*, 186 N.E. at 660.

the insider with whom he traded. In derivative litigation, by contrast, the cause of action belongs to the corporation and any recovery typically goes into the corporate treasury rather than directly to the shareholders. One would normally expect the corporation's board or officers to prosecute such suits. Corporate law recognizes, however, that a corporation's managers sometimes may be reluctant to enforce the corporation's rights. This seems especially likely when the prospective defendant is a fellow director or officer. The derivative suit evolved to deal with such situations, providing a procedural device for shareholders to enforce rights belonging to the corporation.

In *Diamond v. Oreamuno*,[16] the leading insider trading derivative case, defendants Oreamuno and Gonzalez were respectively the Chairman of the Board and President of Management Assistance, Inc. ("MAI"). MAI was in the computer leasing business. It sub-contracted maintenance of leased systems to IBM. As a result of an increase in IBM's charges, MAI's earnings fell precipitously. Before these facts were made public, Oreamuno and Gonzalez sold off 56,500 shares of MAI stock at the then-prevailing price of $28 per share. Once the information was made public, MAI's stock price fell to $11 per share. A shareholder sued derivatively, seeking an order that defendants disgorge their allegedly ill-gotten gains to the corporation.[17] The

16. 248 N.E.2d 910 (N.Y. 1969).

17. In everyday speech, the word "profit" connotes having more money than you started out with. Not so in the world of

court held that a derivative suit was proper in this context and, moreover, that insider trading by corporate officers and directors violated their fiduciary duties to the corporation.[18]

Diamond has been a law professor favorite ever since it was decided. A plethora of law review articles have been written on it, mostly in a favorable vein. *Diamond* also still shows up in most corporations case books. In the real world, however, *Diamond* has proven quite controversial. A number of leading opinions in other jurisdictions have squarely rejected its holdings.[19]

insider trading, where it is possible to profit by avoiding a loss. Courts have treated the use of inside information to avoid a loss as legally indistinguishable from the use of inside information to make a profit in the more conventional sense.

18. There is a procedural oddity inherent in *Diamond*'s willingness to permit derivative suits against inside traders. As is generally the case in corporate law, New York only allows shareholders to bring a derivative suit if they meet the so-called continuing shareholder test: they held stock at the time the wrong was committed, suit was filed, and judgment reached. In cases like *Diamond*, in which outsiders bought the selling insiders' shares, the purchasers were not shareholders until after the wrong was committed. In the flip category of cases, those in which insiders buy from existing shareholders, the sellers (if they sold all their shares) are no longer shareholders. The effect of the continuing shareholder rule should be obvious: no shareholder in the class most would regard as the inside trader's principal victims can serve as a named plaintiff in a *Diamond*-type suit. Where insiders buy, moreover, the allegedly injured selling shareholders cannot even share in any benefit that might flow from a successful derivative suit.

19. See, e.g., *Freeman v. Decio*, 584 F.2d 186 (7th Cir.1978) (Indiana law); *Schein v. Chasen*, 313 So.2d 739, 746 (Fla.1975).

Why has *Diamond* proven so controversial? No one contends that officers or directors never can be held liable for using information learned in their corporate capacities for personal profit. An officer who uses information learned on the job to compete with his corporate employer, or to usurp a corporate opportunity, for example, readily can be held liable for doing so. Insider trading differs in an important way from these cases, however. Recall that derivative litigation is intended to redress an injury to the corporate entity. Where an employee uses inside information to compete with her corporate employer, the injury to the employer is obvious. In *Diamond*, however, the employees did not use their knowledge to compete with the firm, but rather to trade in its securities. The injury, if any, to the corporation is far less obvious in such cases. Unlike most types of tangible property, information can be used by more than one person without necessarily lowering its value. If an officer who has just negotiated a major contract for her corporation thereafter buys some of the firm's stock, for example, it is far from obvious that her trading necessarily reduced the contract's value to the firm.

The *Diamond* court relied on two purportedly analogous precedents to justify allowing a derivative cause of action against inside traders: The Delaware Chancery court's decision in *Brophy v. Cities Service Co.*[20] and the law of agency. On close examination, however, neither provides very much support for *Diamond*.

20. 70 A.2d 5 (Del.Ch.1949).

In *Brophy,* the defendant insider traded on the basis of information about a stock repurchase program the corporation was about to undertake. In a very real sense, the insider was competing with the corporation, which both agency law and corporate law clearly proscribe. While the *Brophy* court did not require a showing of corporate injury, the insider's conduct in fact directly threatened the corporation's interests. If his purchases caused a rise in the stock price, the corporation would be injured by having to pay more for its own purchases. In contrast, the *Diamond* insiders' conduct involved neither competition with the corporation nor a direct threat of harm to it. The information in question related to a historical fact. As such, it simply was not information MAI could use. Indeed, the only imaginable use to which MAI could put this information would be to itself buy or sell its own securities before announcing the decline in earnings. Under the federal securities laws, however, MAI could not lawfully make such trades.

The *Diamond* court made two moves to evade this problem. First, it asserted that proof of injury was not legally necessary, which seems inconsistent with the notion that derivative suits are a vehicle for redressing injuries done to the corporation. Second, the court inferred that MAI might have suffered some harm as a result of the defendants' conduct, even though the complaint failed to allege any such harm. In particular, the court surmised that the defendants' conduct might have injured MAI's reputation. As we shall see in Chapter 4, however, this is not a very likely source of corporate injury. Accordingly, it is quite easy to distinguish *Brophy* from *Diamond*.

Agency law proves an equally problematic justification for the *Diamond* result. According to the Restatement (Second) of Agency, the principal-agent relationship is a fiduciary one with respect to matters within the scope of the agency relationship. More to the point for present purposes, Section 388 of the Agency Restatement imposes a duty on agents to account for profits made in connection with transactions conducted on the principal's behalf. The comments to that section further expand this duty's scope, requiring the agent to account for any profits made by the use of confidential information even if the principal is not harmed by the agent's use of the information. Section 395 provides that an agent may not use for personal gain any information "given him by the principal or acquired by him during the course of or on account of his agency."

One can plausibly argue, however, that the apparent bar on insider trading created by agency law is not as strict as it first appears. The broad prohibition of self-dealing in confidential information appears solely in the comments to Sections 388 and 395. In contrast, the black letter text of Section 388 speaks only of profits made "in connection with transactions conducted by [the agent] on behalf of the principal." One must stretch the phrases "in connection with" and "on behalf of" pretty far in order to reach insider trading profits. Similarly,

Section 395, which speaks directly to the issue of self-dealing in confidential information, only prohibits the use of confidential information for personal gain "in competition with or to the injury of the principal." Arguably, agency law thus requires an injury to the principal before insider trading liability can be imposed.

This argument is supported by *Freeman v. Decio*,[21] the leading case rejecting *Diamond*'s approach. In *Freeman*, the court noted both *Diamond* and the comments to Sections 388 and 395, but nonetheless held that corporate officers and directors could not be held liable for insider trading as a matter of state corporate law without a showing that the corporation was injured by their conduct. *Freeman* conceded that if all confidential information relating to the firm were viewed as a corporate asset, plaintiffs would not need to show an injury to the corporation in order for the insider's trades to constitute a breach of duty. The court said, however, such a view puts the cart before the horse. One should first ask whether there was any potential loss to the corporation before deciding whether or not to treat the information in question as a firm asset. The court further concluded that most instances of insider trading did not pose any cognizable risk of injury to the firm. According to the court, any harm caused by insider trading was borne mainly by the investors with whom the insider trades, rather than the firm. Unlike *Brophy*, moreover, there was no competition with the firm

21.   584 F.2d 186 (7th Cir.1978).

or loss of a corporate opportunity, because there was no profitable use to which the corporation could have lawfully put this information.

Which of these cases was correctly decided as a matter of public policy? Unfortunately, we are not yet ready to decide between *Diamond* and *Freeman*. The basic issue that divides them is whether or not all confidential information relating to the firm is treated as a corporate asset. Put another way, did MAI have a protected property right in all such information? Answering that question is a task best deferred until the penultimate chapter of this text, *Why Do We Care?*, in which we'll look at the allocation of property rights in information.

The Federal Insider Trading Prohibition: Statutory Background

The modern federal insider trading prohibition has its statutory basis in the federal securities laws—principally the Securities Exchange Act of 1934. As with the other New Deal-era securities laws, the Exchange Act was a response to the 1929 stock market crash and the subsequent depression. Congress hoped these laws would ameliorate the economic crisis caused by the crash. Towards that end, all of the various statutes shared two basic purposes: protecting investors engaged in securities transactions and assuring public confidence in the integrity of the securities markets.

From the beginning, disclosure was Congress' favorite tool for regulating securities. As the Supreme Court later stated, the federal securities statutes' fundamental aim was "to substitute a philosophy of full disclosure for the philosophy of *caveat emptor* and thus achieve a high standard of business ethics in the securities industry."[22] Accordingly, prohibitions of fraud and manipulation in connection with the purchase or sale of securities buttressed the Exchange Act's disclosure requirements.

Is insider trading a breach of the disclosure obligations created by the Exchange Act? If not, is it otherwise captured by the Act's prohibition of fraud and manipulation? The United States Supreme Court, among others, thinks so: "A significant purpose of the Exchange Act was to eliminate the idea that use of inside information for personal advantage was a normal emolument of corporate office."[23] Careful examination of the relevant legislative history, however, suggests that regulating insider trading was not one of the Exchange Act's original purposes.[24]

The core of the modern federal insider trading prohibition derives its statutory authority from § 10(b) of the Exchange Act, which provides in pertinent part that:

22. *SEC v. Capital Gains Research Bureau, Inc.*, 375 U.S. 180, 186 (1963).

23. *Dirks v. SEC*, 463 U.S. 646, 653 n. 10 (1983).

24. See generally Stephen M. Bainbridge, *Incorporating State Law Fiduciary Duties into the Federal Insider Trading Prohibition*, 52 Wash & Lee L. Rev. 1189, 1228–1237 (1995); Michael P. Dooley, *Enforcement of Insider Trading Restrictions*, 66 Va. L. Rev. 1, 55–69 (1980); Frank H. Easterbrook, *Insider Trading Secret Agents, Evidentiary Privileges, and the Production of Information*, 1981 Sup. Ct. Rev. 309, 317–20.

It shall be unlawful for any person, directly or indirectly, by the use of any means or instrumentality of interstate commerce or of the mails, or of any facility of any national securities exchange—

(b) To use or employ, in connection with the purchase or sale of any security registered on a national securities exchange or any security not so registered, any manipulative or deceptive device or contrivance in contravention of such rules and regulations as the SEC may prescribe as necessary or appropriate in the public interest or for the protection of investors.

Notice two things about this text. First, it doesn't actually make anything illegal. Put more formally, § 10(b) is not self-executing. It grants authority to the SEC to prohibit "any manipulative or deceptive device or contrivance" and then makes the use of such proscribed devices illegal. Until the SEC exercises its rulemaking authority, however, the statute is wholly ineffectual.

The second point to be noticed is the absence of the word "insider." Nothing in § 10(b) explicitly proscribes insider trading. To be sure, § 10(b) often is described as a catchall intended to capture various types of securities fraud not expressly covered by more specific provisions of the Exchange Act.[25] What the SEC catches under § 10(b), however, must not only be fraud, but also within the scope of the authority delegated to it by Congress.[26] Section

25. *Chiarella v. United States*, 445 U.S. 222, 234–35 (1980).

26. *Ernst & Ernst v. Hochfelder*, 425 U.S. 185, 212–14 (1976).

10(b) received little attention during the hearings on the Exchange Act and apparently was seen simply as a grant of authority to the SEC to prohibit manipulative devices not covered by § 9. As Thomas Corcoran, a prominent member of President Roosevelt's administration and leader of the Exchange Act's supporters, put it: § 10(b) was intended to prohibit the invention of "any other cunning devices" besides those prohibited by other sections.[27] Only a single passage, albeit an oft-cited one, in the Exchange Act's voluminous legislative history directly indicates insider trading was one of those cunning devices: "Among the most vicious practices unearthed at the hearings ... was the flagrant betrayal of their fiduciary duties by directors and officers of corporations who used their positions of trust and the confidential information which came to them in such positions, to aid them in their market activities."[28] In context, however, this passage does not deal with insider trading as we understand the term today, but rather with manipulation of stock prices by pools of insiders and speculators through cross sales, wash sales, and similar "cunning" methods.[29] Nothing else in the legislative history suggests that Congress intended § 10(b) to create a sweeping prohibition of insider trading.

27. Stock Exchange Regulation: Hearing on H.R. 7852 and H.R. 8720 Before the House Comm. on Interstate and Foreign Commerce, 73d Cong., 2d Sess. 115 (1934).

28. S. Rep. No. 1455, 73d Cong., 2d Sess. 55 (1934).

29. Dooley, supra note 24, at 56 n.235.

To the extent the 1934 Congress addressed insider trading, it did so not through § 10(b), but rather through § 16(b), which permits the issuer of affected securities to recover insider short-swing profits. As we'll see in Chapter 5, § 16(b) imposes quite limited restrictions on insider trading. It does not reach transactions occurring more than six months apart, nor does it apply to persons other than those named in the statute or to transactions in securities not registered under § 12. Indeed, some have argued that § 16(b) was not even intended to deal with insider trading, but rather with manipulation.[30] In any event, given that Congress could have struck at insider trading both more directly and forcefully, and given that Congress chose not to do so, § 16(b) offers no statutory justification for the more sweeping prohibition under § 10(b).

If Congress had intended in 1934 that the SEC use § 10(b) to craft a sweeping prohibition on insider trading, moreover, the SEC was quite dilatory in doing so. Rule 10b–5, the foundation on which the modern insider trading prohibition rests, was not promulgated until 1942, eight years after the Exchange Act passed Congress. The Rule provides:

> It shall be unlawful for any person, directly or indirectly, by the use of any means or instrumentality of interstate commerce, or of the mails or of any facility of any national securities exchange,
>
> (a) To employ any device, scheme, or artifice to defraud,

30. Dooley, supra note 24, at 56–58.

(b) To make any untrue statement of a material fact or to omit to state a material fact necessary in order to make the statements made, in the light of the circumstances under which they were made, not misleading, or

(c) To engage in any act, practice, or course of business which operates or would operate as a fraud or deceit upon any person, in connection with the purchase or sale of any security.

Note that, as with § 10(b) itself, the rule on its face does not prohibit (or even speak to) insider trading. Nor was Rule 10b–5 initially used against insider trading on public secondary trading markets. Instead, like state common law, the initial Rule 10b–5 cases were limited to face-to-face and/or control transactions. Not until 1961 did the SEC finally conclude that insider trading on an impersonal stock exchange violated Rule 10b–5.[31] Only then did the modern federal insider trading prohibition at last begin to take shape.

In sum, the modern prohibition is a creature of SEC administrative actions and judicial opinions, only loosely tied to the statutory language and its legislative history. U.S. Supreme Court Chief Justice William Rehnquist famously observed that Rule 10b–5 is "a judicial oak which has grown from little more than a legislative acorn."[32] Nowhere in Rule 10b–5 jurisprudence is this truer than where the insider trading prohibition is concerned, given the

31. 40 S.E.C. 907 (1961).

32. *Blue Chip Stamps v. Manor Drug Stores*, 421 U.S. 723, 737 (1975).

tiny (even nonexistent) legislative acorn on which it rests. As a former SEC solicitor once admitted, the "[m]odern development of the law of insider trading is a classic example of common law in the federal courts."[33]

Digression: A Rule 10b–5 Primer

Before tracing the evolution of the insider trading prohibition under Rule 10b–5, however, a brief overview of the rule itself is in order. The rule's three subsections outlaw three types of conduct in connection with the purchase or sale of a security: the use of any device, scheme or artifice to defraud; material misstatements and omissions; and any act, practice or course of business that operates as a fraud. In general, however, the differences (if any) between the various rule's subsections do not matter very much—Rule 10b–5 is generally treated as broad prohibition of fraud in securities transactions and no one cares very much about whether the conduct in question is an artifice to defraud or a practice that operates as a fraud.

On its face, the rule does not tell us very much other than that fraud in connection with securities transactions is a bad thing. What elements does one have to prove in order to show a violation of the rule? Who has standing to sue violators? What remedies can they seek? Few of these questions are answered by the plain text of the rule (or the

33. Paul Gonson & David E. Butler, *In Wake of "Dirks," Courts Debate Definition of "Insider,"* Legal Times, Apr. 2, 1984, at 16, col. 1.

statute, for that matter).[34] Instead, these issues have been worked out in a long series of decisions, including a number of important Supreme Court decisions.

Standing. Both the United States Justice Department (typically acting through local U.S. Attorney's offices) and the SEC clearly have standing to sue those who violate Rule 10b–5. The more interesting question is whether private parties have standing to sue under the rule. Nothing in either the rule or the statute explicitly authorizes such a private party cause of action. Lower federal courts recognized an implied right of action under Rule 10b–5 as early as 1946,[35] however, and the Supreme Court followed suit in 1971.[36] Today, of course, judicial implication of private rights of action is highly controversial and the current Supreme Court seems less inclined to create or preserve such rights of action than any of its recent predecessors. The private right of action under Rule 10b–5 neverthe-

---

34. Both the statute and the rule plainly require a jurisdictional nexus: there must be a use of a means or instrumentality of interstate commerce, the mails, or any facility of a national securities exchange in order for the statute to be applicable. In most cases, this requirement is easily satisfied: basically, if the defendant made a phone call or sent a letter in connection with the fraud, § 10(b) can apply. Section 10(b) will also apply if the defendant takes either of those steps indirectly; for example, if the defendant orders his broker to sell shares, and the broker uses the phone or the mails, the statute is triggered.

35. *Kardon v. Nat'l Gypsum Co.*, 69 F.Supp. 512 (E.D.Pa. 1946).

36. *Superintendent of Insurance v. Bankers Life & Cas. Co.*, 404 U.S. 6, 13 n. 9 (1971).

less remains quite firmly established. As former Justice Thurgood Marshall once observed, the "existence of this implied remedy is simply beyond peradventure."[37]

Although the Supreme Court has confirmed the implied right of action under Rule 10b–5, it has limited private party standing to persons who actually buy or sell a security.[38] This may seem trivial or obvious, but in fact it is not. Suppose the executives of a company wanted to drive down the price of the firm's stock so that they could buy it for themselves. They put out false bad news about the company. You were considering buying stock in the company but were dissuaded by the bad news put out by the executives. If you later try to sue, arguing that but for the executives' misconduct you would have bought some of the company's stock, the Supreme Court's standing rules will bar you from bringing suit.

Although one must have either purchased or sold a security in order to have standing to sue under Rule 10b–5, one need not have purchased or sold in order to be a proper party defendant. In the seminal insider trading case, *SEC v. Texas Gulf Sulphur Co.*,[39] the defendant corporation issued a misleading press release. Because the corporation had neither bought nor sold any securities during the relevant

37. *Herman & MacLean v. Huddleston*, 459 U.S. 375, 380 (1983).

38. *Blue Chip Stamps v. Manor Drug Stores*, 421 U.S. 723 (1975).

39. 401 F.2d 833 (2d Cir.1968), cert. denied, 394 U.S. 976 (1969).

time period, it argued that it could not be held liable under Rule 10b–5. The court rejected this argument, observing that Rule 10b–5 on its face prohibits fraud "in connection with the purchase or sale of any security." The court interpreted this language as requiring "only that the device employed, whatever it might be, be of a sort that would cause reasonable investors to rely thereon, and, in connection therewith, so relying, cause them to purchase or sell a corporation's securities."

Although the Rule 10b–5 implied right of action long has been a major weapon in the arsenal of defrauded investors, it is less important in insider trading than in other contexts. First, private party litigation against inside traders is rare—at least compared to other types of securities fraud—and is usually parasitic on SEC enforcement actions. Second, Congress has created a special express cause of action for those who trade contemporaneously with inside traders. Our discussion of Rule 10b–5's elements thus can focus on those applicable to actions brought by the government.

Application to Omission Cases. Rule 10b–5 applies to both affirmative misrepresentations and passive omissions. For our purposes, however, issues relating to omissions are far more important than those relating to misrepresentations. Most insider trading cases today involve trading on impersonal stock exchanges in which the alleged inside trader is accused of having bought or sold stock without first disclosing nonpublic information she knew when she traded.

Two aspects of Rule 10b–5, as applied to omission cases, are especially important. First, not all omissions give rise to liability. Instead, liability can be imposed only if the defendant had a duty to speak. As we shall see, this requirement has been the central feature of the Supreme Court's insider trading jurisprudence. Second, reliance and transaction causation are presumed in omission cases. In private party litigation under Rule 10b–5, plaintiff generally must prove that he or she reasonably relied upon the defendant's fraudulent words or conduct.[40] Plaintiff also must prove both transaction causation and loss causation. The former is analogous to but for causation in tort law—it is a showing that defendant's words or conduct caused plaintiff to engage in the transaction in question. Loss causation is somewhat analogous to the tort law concept of proximate causation—it involves showing that the defendant's words or conduct caused plaintiff's economic loss. In omission cases, both transaction causation and reliance generally are presumed so long as plaintiff can show defendant had a duty to disclose and failed to do so.[41]

40. In some misrepresentation cases, reliance and transaction causation may be presumed under the so-called "fraud on the market" theory. A rebuttable presumption arises under this theory if plaintiff can prove defendant made material public misrepresentations, the security was traded on an efficient market, and plaintiff traded in the security between the time the misrepresentations were made and the truth was revealed. *Basic Inc. v. Levinson*, 485 U.S. 224 (1988).

41. *Affiliated Ute Citizens v. United States*, 406 U.S. 128 (1972).

Materiality. Under Rule 10b–5, only material misrepresentations or omissions are actionable. Materiality is determined by asking whether there is a substantial likelihood that a reasonable investor would consider the information important in deciding how to act. When one is dealing with speculative or contingent facts, of course, this test can be hard to apply. Recall that in *Goodwin v. Agassiz*, for example, the defendants were buying stock on the basis of a theory that land in the area the company worked might have commercially significant copper deposits. At the time the defendants traded, the theory was just that—a theory, which had not been verified. Was it material, as defined by the federal securities law?

In *Basic Inc. v. Levinson*,[42] the Supreme Court adopted what it called "a highly fact-dependent probability/magnitude balancing approach" to materiality in the context of contingent facts. Although Basic in fact was secretly negotiating a possible merger with another company, it issued three public denials that any such negotiations were underway. When the merger was finally announced, a class action was brought on behalf of those investors who had sold Basic stock during the period between the false denials and the merger announcement. The plaintiff class allegedly received a lower price for their shares than would have been the case if Basic had told the truth.

The core issue was whether the denials were material. When the denials were made, it had not

42.   *Basic Inc. v. Levinson*, 485 U.S. 224 (1988).

been certain that the merger would go through. The probability/magnitude balancing test was thus appropriate. As to the probability part of the equation, the court looked to "indicia of interest in the transaction at the highest corporate levels." Evidence such as "board resolutions, instructions to investment bankers, and actual negotiations between principals or their intermediaries may serve as indicia of interest." As to magnitude, the court deemed it quite high, opining that a merger is "the most important event that can occur in a small corporation's life, to wit, its death...." Notice, however, that magnitude appears to have both a relative and an absolute component. A merger of a small company into a large company, for example, is a big deal for the target, but may be insignificant from the acquirer's perspective.

Although the probability/magnitude language sounds technically sophisticated and precise, it is in fact inherently subjective and indeterminate. You may recall the famous Hand Formula from torts—multiply the probability of injury times the magnitude of the likely resulting injury; if the product is less than the benefits of adequate precautions, liability for allegedly negligent conduct may be imposed.[43] At first glance, the *Basic* test sounds like the Hand formula, but on closer examination there is no magic product to serve as a threshold above which information becomes material. The court never tells us how high a probability nor how large

43. See *United States v. Carroll Towing Co.*, 159 F.2d 169 (2d Cir.1947).

a magnitude is necessary for information to be deemed material. One thus inside trades on the basis of speculative information knowing that a jury, acting with the benefit of hindsight, may reach a different conclusion about how probability and magnitude should be balanced than you did.

A major issue in insider trading cases is whether the allegedly illegal insider trading behavior can serve as proof that the facts on which the insider traded were material. The problem, of course, is the potential for bootstrapping: if the allegedly illegal trade proves that the information is material, the materiality requirement becomes meaningless—all information in the defendant's possession when he or she traded would be material. Nonetheless, a footnote in the Supreme Court's *Basic* opinion flatly stated that "trading and profit making by insiders can serve as an indication of materiality."

Scienter. One can easily mislead investors without intending to do so. Even an honest mistake might cause some to be misled. As such, it is not apparent that liability for securities fraud should be premised on intent. Tort law encourages drivers to drive more safely, because they can be held liable for negligent accidents. Tort law also encourages manufacturers to put out safer products by imposing strict liability for defective products. Should securities law be any less rigorous in encouraging accurate disclosure?

Liability in fact can be imposed for unintentional misrepresentations under some securities law provisions. Sections 11 and 12(a)(2) of the 1933 Securities Act, for example, require no evidence from plaintiff with respect to the defendant's state of mind. Instead, state of mind is at most an affirmative defense under these provisions. In order to make out the state of mind defense, moreover, defendants must show that they were non-negligent.

Under Rule 10b–5, however, the Supreme Court has held that plaintiff's prima facie case must include proof defendant acted with scienter, which the court defined as a mental state embracing an intent to deceive, manipulate or defraud.[44] Although this formulation clearly precludes Rule 10b–5 liability for those who are merely negligent, the Supreme Court left open the issue of whether recklessness alone met the scienter requirement. Subsequent lower court decisions have generally held that recklessness suffices.

The Limits of Rule 10b–5: The Need for Deception. In *Santa Fe Industries, Inc. v. Green*,[45] Santa Fe effected a short-form merger with a subsidiary corporation. Minority shareholders of the subsidiary were dissatisfied with the consideration they were paid for their stock. Although plaintiffs had state law remedies, such as the statutory appraisal proceeding, they opted to sue under Rule 10b–5. Plaintiffs claimed that the merger violated 10b–5 because it was effected without prior notice

44. *Aaron v. SEC*, 446 U.S. 680 (1980); *Ernst & Ernst v. Hochfelder*, 425 U.S. 185 (1976).

45. 430 U.S. 462 (1977).

to the minority shareholders and was done without any legitimate business purpose. They also claimed that their shares had been undervalued. Both claims raised, quite directly, the question of what conduct is covered by the rule. The Supreme Court held that plaintiffs had not stated a cause of action under Rule 10b–5.

Drawing on the plain text and legislative history of the rule, the court concluded that a 10b–5 cause of action arises only out of deception or manipulation. Deception requires a misrepresentation or omission. Because the *Santa Fe* plaintiffs received full disclosure, there was no misrepresentation or omission. In addition, neither of plaintiffs' claims went to disclosure violations; rather, both went to the substance of the transaction. Plaintiffs were not claiming that Santa Fe lied to them, but that the transaction was unfair. In other words, they were claiming that a breach of fiduciary duty gives rise to a cause of action under 10b–5. The Supreme Court held that a mere breach of duty will not give rise to liability under 10b–5.

Manipulation is conduct intended to mislead investors by artificially affecting market activity. In other words, defendant must engage in conduct that creates artificial changes in the price of a security or artificially changes the volume of trading in a security. Again, Santa Fe was mainly being charged with a breach of the state law fiduciary duties a majority shareholder owes to minority shareholders. Nothing Santa Fe did constituted unlawful manipulation.

In addition to its textual arguments, the Supreme Court also relied on policy considerations grounded in federalism. The court clearly was concerned that allowing plaintiffs to go forward in this case would federalize much of state corporate law, in many cases overriding well-established state policies of corporate regulation. In the court's view, if the *Santa Fe* plaintiffs were allowed to sue, every breach of fiduciary duty case would give rise to a federal claim under Rule 10b–5. The court refused to give the Rule 10b–5 such an expansive reach, instead holding that it did not reach "transactions which constitute no more than internal corporate mismanagement."[46]

Santa Fe was a critical holding in Rule 10b–5's evolution, putting the substantive fairness of a transaction outside the rule's scope. The rule henceforth was limited to disclosure violations. *Santa Fe* also implied a second—and potentially even more significant—constraint on the rule in suggesting that misconduct covered by state corporate law should be left to state law. As we have seen, insider trading long has fallen within the regulatory purview of state corporate law. As such, *Santa Fe* could have (and perhaps should have) constrained much of the federal insider trading prohibition's growth. As we shall see, however, later courts have largely ducked this issue.

Secondary Liability and the Plain Meaning Issue. In *Central Bank of Denver v. First Interstate*

46. Id. at 479.

Bank,[47] the Supreme Court held that there was no
implied private right of action against those who aid
and abet violations of Rule 10b–5. *Central Bank*
thus substantially limited the scope of secondary
liability under the rule, at least insofar as private
party causes of action are concerned. For our purposes, however, the case is more significant for its
methodology than its holding.

Until quite recently, Rule 10b–5 was regarded as
an example of interstitial lawmaking in which the
courts used common-law adjudicatory methods to
flesh out the text's bare bones. In *Central Bank*,
however, the court held the scope of conduct prohibited by § 10(b) (and thus the rule) is controlled
by the text of the statute. Where the plain text does
not resolve some aspect of the Rule 10b–5 cause of
action, courts must "infer 'how the 1934 Congress
would have addressed the issue had the 10b–5 action been included as an express provision of the
1934 Act.' " The court elsewhere acknowledged this
to be an "awkward task," but Justice Scalia put it
more colorfully: "We are imagining here."[48] *Central
Bank* constrained this imaginative process by requiring courts to "use the express causes of action
in the securities acts as the primary model for the
§ 10(b) action."[49] As we shall see, *Central Bank*
poses a significant threat to the further evolution of

47.   511 U.S. 164 (1994).

48.   *Lampf, Pleva, Lipkind, Prupis & Petigrow v. Gilbertson*,
501 U.S. 350 (1991).

49.   *Central Bank*, 511 U.S. at 178.

the federal insider trading prohibition, although thus far its potential remains unrealized.

The Federal Insider Trading Prohibition: Common Law Origins

The modern federal insider trading prohibition fairly can be said to have begun with the SEC's enforcement action *In re Cady, Roberts & Co.*[50] Curtiss–Wright Corporation's board of directors decided to reduce the company's quarterly dividend. One of the directors, J. Cheever Cowdin, was also a partner in Cady, Roberts & Co., a stock brokerage firm. Before the news was announced, Cowdin informed one of his partners, Robert M. Gintel, of the impending dividend cut. Gintel then sold several thousand shares of Curtiss–Wright stock held in customer accounts over which he had discretionary trading authority. When the dividend cut was announced, Curtiss–Wright's stock price fell several dollars per share. Gintel's customers thus avoided substantial losses.

Cady, Roberts involved what is now known as tipping: an insider (the tipper) who knows confidential information does not himself trade, but rather informs (tips) someone else (the tippee) who does trade. It also involved trading on an impersonal stock exchange, instead of a face-to-face transaction. As the SEC acknowledged, this made *Cady, Roberts* a case of first impression. Prior 10b–5 cases in which inside information was used for personal gain had involved issues of tortious fraudulent conceal-

50. 40 S.E.C. 907 (1961).

ment little different from the sorts of cases with which the state common law had dealt. Notwithstanding that limitation, the SEC held that Gintel had violated Rule 10b–5. In so doing, it articulated what became known as the "disclose or abstain" rule: An insider in possession of material nonpublic information must disclose such information before trading or, if disclosure is impossible or improper, abstain from trading.

It was not immediately clear what precedential value *Cady, Roberts* would have. It was an administrative ruling by the SEC, not a judicial opinion. It involved a regulated industry closely supervised by the SEC. There was the long line of precedent, represented by *Goodwin v. Agassiz*, to the contrary. In short order, however, the basic *Cady, Roberts* principles became the law of the land.

Texas Gulf Sulphur

In March of 1959, agents of Texas Gulf Sulphur Co. (TGS) found evidence of an ore deposit near Timmons, Ontario. In October 1963, Texas Gulf Sulphur began ground surveys of the area. In early November, a drilling rig took core samples from depths of several hundred feet. Visual examination of the samples suggested commercially significant deposits of copper and zinc. TGS's president ordered the exploration group to maintain strict confidentiality, even to the point of withholding the news from other TGS directors and employees. In early December, a chemical assay confirmed the presence of copper, zinc, and silver. At the subsequent trial, several expert witnesses testified that they had never heard of any other initial exploratory drill hole showing comparable results. Over the next several months, TGS acquired the rights to the land under which this remarkable ore deposit lay. In March and early April 1964, further drilling confirmed that TGS had made a significant ore discovery. After denying several rumors about the find, TGS finally announced its discovery in a press conference on April 16, 1964.

Throughout the fall of 1963 and spring of 1964, a number of TGS insiders bought stock and/or options on company stock. Others tipped off outsiders. Still others accepted stock options authorized by the company's board of directors without informing the directors of the discovery. Between November 1963 and March 1964, the insiders were able to buy at prices that were slowly rising, albeit with fluctuations, from just under $18 per share to $25 per share. As rumors began circulating in late March and early April, the price jumped to about $30 per share. On April 16th, the stock opened at $31, but quickly jumped to $37 per share. By May 15, 1964, TGS's stock was trading at over $58 per share—a 222% rise over the previous November's price. Any joy the insiders may taken from their profits was short-lived, however, as the SEC sued them for violating Rule 10b–5.

Texas Gulf Sulphur is the first of the truly seminal insider trading cases. It is still in most of the case books, in large part because it presents such a stark and classic fact pattern. In examining *Texas Gulf Sulphur*, however, it is critical to distinguish between what the law *was* and what the law *is*— although much of what was said in that opinion is still valid, the core insider trading holding is no longer good law.

The Second Circuit Court of Appeals held that an insider possessing material nonpublic information the insider must either disclose such information before trading or abstain from trading until the information has been disclosed.[51] Thus was born

51. In a case like *Texas Gulf Sulphur*, it is just as important to determine when the information in question became material as it is to determine whether the information was material. Consider how the materiality standard would apply at two critical dates: November 12, when the visual assay indicated a potentially significant ore strike, and April 7, when the results of additional test holes confirmed that mining would be commercially viable. To review, materiality is now defined by whether there is a substantial likelihood that a reasonable investor would consider the omitted fact important in deciding whether to buy or sell securities. Where a fact is contingent or speculative, moreover, materiality is determined by balancing the indicated probability that the event will occur and the anticipated magnitude of the event in light of the totality of the company's activity.

Under these standards, the ore discovery was certainly material as of April 7. The additional test holes had confirmed that the initial core sample was not an aberration—TGS really had a major find on its hands. After April 7, the critical issue is not whether the strike will pay off, but when. The balancing test thus is not at issue, because we are no longer dealing with a contingent fact. Given the size of the discovery, this was certainly information any reasonable investor would consider significant.

It is less clear that the information known on November 12th would be regarded as material as of that date. Before April there was only one core sample. While that sample was remarkable, what is now known as the "disclose or abstain" rule.

The name is something of a misnomer, of course. The court presumably phrased the rule in terms of disclosure because this was an omissions case under Rule 10b–5. Recall that in such cases the defendant must owe a duty of disclosure to some investor in order for liability to be imposed. As a practical matter, however, disclosure will rarely be an option.

During the relevant time period, TGS had no affirmative duty to disclose the ore strike. As the Second Circuit correctly noted, the timing of disclosure is a matter for the business judgment of corporate managers, subject to any affirmative disclosure requirements imposed by the stock exchanges or the SEC. In this case, moreover, a valuable corporate purpose was served by delaying disclosure: confidentiality prevented competitors from buying up the mineral rights and kept down the price landowners would charge for them. The company therefore had no duty to disclose the discovery, at

only a highly trained geologist would be able to draw conclusions from it. Since it would take a highly sophisticated investor with considerable expertise in mining operations to understand the relevance of the find, perhaps the hypothetical reasonable investor would not consider it important. (But see the testimony of a stock broker who opined that one good test hole was a signal to buy mining stock.)

One might also consider the response of the company and the insiders. The firm's decision to acquire options on the surrounding land tends to point towards a finding of materiality. According to the court, so did the insiders' own trading conduct, although we have seen that this is a somewhat dubious position in view of the resulting bootstrapping effect.

least up until the time that the land acquisition program was completed.

Given that the corporation had no duty to disclose, and had decided not to disclose the information, the insiders' fiduciary duties to the corporation would preclude them disclosing it for personal gain. In this case, the company's president had specifically instructed insiders in the know to keep the information confidential, but such an instruction was not technically necessary. Agency law precludes a firm's agents from disclosing confidential information that belongs to their corporate principal, as all information relating to the ore strike clearly did.

Disclosure by an insider who wishes to trade thus is only feasible if there is no legitimate corporate purpose for maintaining secrecy. These situations, however, presumably will be relatively rare—it is hard to imagine many business developments that can be disclosed immediately without working some harm to the corporation. In most cases, the disclose or abstain rule really does not provide the insider with a disclosure option: generally the duty will be one of complete abstention.

The policy foundation on which the Second Circuit erected the disclose or abstain rule was equality of access to information. The court contended that the federal insider trading prohibition was intended to assure that "all investors trading on impersonal exchanges have relatively equal access to material information."[52] Put another way, the majority thought Congress intended "that all members of the investing public should be subject to identical market risks."

The equality of access principle admittedly has some intuitive appeal. As we shall see, the SEC consistently has tried to maintain it as the basis of insider trading liability. Many commentators still endorse it on fairness grounds. The implications of the equal access principle become troubling when we start dealing with attenuated circumstances, however, especially with respect to market information.[53] Suppose a representative of TGS had

52. *SEC v. Texas Gulf Sulphur Co.*, 401 F.2d 833 (2d Cir. 1968), cert. denied, 394 U.S. 976 (1969).

53. All sorts of information can effect the price of a company's stock. Suppose you receive two hot tips. One is from an insider of Acme Company, who tells you that Acme is about to announce a major new contract, which is expected to significantly increase Acme's earnings. The other is from a law school classmate who is a lawyer for Ajax Corporation, who tells you that Ajax is about to make a hostile takeover bid for Acme. Recognizing that both tips are good news for Acme's stock, you buy 1000 shares. You are found out and charged with illegal insider trading. These examples capture the distinction between inside and market information. Market information is commonly defined as information about events or developments that affect the market for a company's securities, but not the company's assets or earnings. It typically emanates from noncorporate sources and deals primarily with information affecting the trading markets for the corporation's securities. Inside information typically comes from internal corporate sources and involves events or developments affecting the issuer's assets or earnings. The tip about Ajax's takeover bid thus involved market information, while the tip about the new contract involved inside information. Although this distinction can be helpful, and is often drawn in the literature and cases, it is not dispositive as a legal approached a landowner in the Timmons area to negotiate purchasing the mineral rights to the land. TGS's agent does not disclose the ore strike, but the landowner turns out to be pretty smart. She knows TGS has been drilling in the area and has heard rumors that it has been buying up a lot of mineral rights. She puts two and two together, reaches the obvious conclusion, and buys some TGS stock. Under a literal reading of *Texas Gulf Sulphur*, has our landowner committed illegal insider trading?

The surprising answer is "probably." The *Texas Gulf Sulphur* court stated that the insider trading prohibition applies to "anyone in possession of material inside information," because § 10(b) was intended to assure that "all investors trading on impersonal exchanges have relatively equal access to material information." The court further stated that the prohibition applies to anyone who has "access, directly or *indirectly*" to confidential information (here is the sticking point) if he or she knows that the information is unavailable to the investing public. The only issue thus perhaps would be a factual one turning on the landowner's state of mind: did she know she was dealing with confidential information. If so, the equal access policy would seem to justify imposing a duty on her. Query whether the insider trading prohibition should stretch quite that far. As it continued to develop, some significant shrinking in fact took place, but that is a story for the next chapter.

matter. Assuming the other prerequisites for insider trading liability are satisfied, you can go to jail just as easily for trading on market information as inside information.

CHAPTER 3

THE MODERN FEDERAL INSIDER TRADING PROHIBITION

Although *Strong v. Repide* gave the United States Supreme Court an early start on insider trading, the prohibition developed without further assistance from the court for over seven decades. In the 1980s, however, the court issued two decisions—*Chiarella v. United States*[54] and *Dirks v. SEC*[55]—that significantly cut back on the scope of *Texas Gulf Sulphur*'s disclose or abstain rule. In response, the SEC developed two new theories of liability—the misappropriation theory and Rule 14e–3—that recaptured much, but not all, of the ground it lost in *Chiarella* and *Dirks*. Both theories were upheld by the Supreme Court in its recent *United States v. O'Hagan*[56] decision. Evaluating an insider trading case thus now requires one to consider three distinct theories of liability (not counting § 16(b)). This chapter takes them up in turn.

Chiarella v. United States

Vincent Chiarella was an employee of Pandick Press, a financial printer that prepared tender offer

54. 445 U.S. 222 (1980).

55. 463 U.S. 646 (1983).

56. 521 U.S. 642 (1997).

disclosure materials, among other documents. In preparing those materials Pandick used codes to conceal the names of the companies involved, but Chiarella broke the codes. He purchased target company shares before the bid was announced, then sold the shares for considerable profits after announcement of the bid.

Chiarella was one of the first of a series of high profile takeover-related insider trading cases during the 1980s. Obviously, one can significantly increase takeover profits if one knows in advance that a takeover will be forthcoming. If you know of an impending bid prior to its announcement, you can buy up stock at the low pre-announcement price and sell or tender at the higher post-announcement price. The earlier one knows of the bid, of course, the greater the spread between your purchase and sale prices and the greater the resulting profit. By using options, rather than actually buying target stock, you can further increase your profits, because options permit one to control larger blocks of stock for the same investment. During the 1980s, a number of Wall Street takeover players—among whom Dennis Levine, Ivan Boesky, and Michael Milken are the best-known—allegedly added millions of illegally gained insider trading dollars to the already vast fortunes they realized from more legitimate takeover activity.[57]

57. The volatile mix of takeovers and insider trading is entertainingly depicted in Oliver Stone's movie *Wall Street* (1987). For a fascinating popular history of the 1980s insider trading scandals, see JAMES B. STEWART, DEN OF THIEVES (1991). For a spirited defense of Milken and his ilk, see DANIEL R. FISCHEL,

Relative to some of those who followed him into federal court, Vincent Chiarella was small fry. But his case produced the first landmark Supreme Court insider trading ruling since *Strong v. Repide*.[58] Chiarella was convicted of violating Rule 10b–5 by trading on the basis of material nonpublic information. The Second Circuit affirmed his conviction, applying the same equality of access to information-based disclose or abstain rule it had created in *Texas Gulf Sulphur*. Under the equal access-based standard, Chiarella clearly loses: he had greater access to information than those with whom he traded. But notice: Chiarella was not an employee, officer, or director of any of the companies in whose stock he traded. He worked solely for Pandick Press, which in turn was not an agent of any of those companies. Pandick worked for acquiring companies—not the takeover targets in whose stock Chiarella traded.

Chiarella's conviction demonstrated how far the federal insider trading prohibition had departed from its state common law predecessors. Recall that state common law had required, where it imposed liability at all, a fiduciary relationship between buyer and seller. The mere fact that one party had more information than the other was not grounds for setting aside the transaction or imposing damages. Yet, it was for that reason alone that the Second Circuit upheld Chiarella's conviction.

Payback: The Conspiracy to Destroy Michael Milken and His Financial Revolution (1995).

58. *Chiarella v. United States*, 445 U.S. 222 (1980).

The Supreme Court reversed. In doing so, the court squarely rejected the notion that § 10(b) was intended to assure all investors equal access to information. The Court said it could not affirm Chiarella's conviction without recognizing a general duty between all participants in market transactions to forego trades based on material, nonpublic information, and it refused to impose such a duty.

Chiarella thus made clear that the disclose or abstain rule is not triggered merely because the trader possesses material nonpublic information. When a 10b–5 action is based upon nondisclosure, there can be no fraud absent a duty to speak, and no such duty arises from the mere possession of nonpublic information. Instead, the disclose or abstain theory of liability for insider trading was now premised on the inside trader being subject to a duty to disclose to the party on the other side of the transaction that arose from a relationship of trust and confidence between the parties thereto.

Chiarella radically limited the scope of the insider trading prohibition as it had been defined in *Texas Gulf Sulphur*. Consider the landowner hypothetical discussed in the last chapter: Under an equal access to information-based standard, she is liable for insider trading because she had material information unavailable to those with whom she traded. Under *Chiarella*, however, she cannot be held liable. She is (by hypothesis) not the agent or fiduciary of TGS shareholders and, presumably, has no other special relationship of trust and confidence with them. Accordingly, she is free to trade on the basis of what she knows without fear of liability. The policy conundrum is now flipped, of course: after *Texas Gulf Sulphur*, the question was how large a net should the prohibition cast; after *Chiarella*, the question was how broad should be the scope of immunity created by the new fiduciary relationship requirement.

Dirks v. SEC

Raymond Dirks was a securities analyst who uncovered the massive Equity Funding of America fraud. Dirks first began investigating Equity Funding after receiving allegations from Ronald Secrist, a former officer of Equity Funding, that the corporation was engaged in widespread fraudulent corporate practices. Dirks passed the results of his investigation to the SEC and the Wall Street Journal, but also discussed his findings with various clients. A number of those clients sold their holdings of Equity Funding securities before any public disclosure of the fraud, thereby avoiding substantial losses. After the fraud was made public and Equity Funding went into receivership, the SEC began an investigation of Dirk's role in exposing the fraud. One might think Dirks deserved a medal (one suspects Mr. Dirks definitely felt that way), but one would be wrong. The SEC censured Dirks for violating the federal insider trading prohibition by repeating the allegations of fraud to his clients.

Under the *Texas Gulf Sulphur* equal access to information standard, tipping of the sort at issue in *Dirks* presented no conceptual problems. The tippee had access to information unavailable to those with whom he traded and, as such, is liable. After *Chiarella*, however, the tipping problem was more complex. Neither Dirks nor any of his customers were agents, officers, or directors of Equity Funding. Nor did they have any other form of special relationship of trust and confidence with those with whom they traded.

In reversing Dirk's censure, the Supreme Court expressly reaffirmed its rejection of the equal access standard and its requirement of a breach of fiduciary duty in order for liability to be imposed:

> We were explicit in *Chiarella* in saying that there can be no duty to disclose where the person who has traded on inside information "was not [the corporation's] agent, ... was not a fiduciary, [or] was not a person in whom the sellers [of the securities] had placed their trust and confidence." Not to require such a fiduciary relationship, we recognized, would "depar[t] radically from the established doctrine that duty arises from a specific relationship between two parties" and would amount to "recognizing a general duty between all participants in market transactions to forgo actions based on material, nonpublic information."[59]

59. *Dirks v. SEC*, 463 U.S. 646, 654–55 (1983).

Recognizing that this formulation posed problems for tipping cases, the court held that a tippee's liability is derivative of that of the tipper, "arising from [the tippee's] role as a participant after the fact in the insider's breach of a fiduciary duty." A tippee therefore can be held liable only when the tipper breached a fiduciary duty by disclosing information to the tippee, and the tippee knows or has reason to know of the breach of duty.

On the *Dirks* facts, this formulation precluded imposition of liability. To be sure, Secrist was an employee and, hence, a fiduciary of Equity Funding. But the mere fact that an insider tips nonpublic information is not enough under *Dirks*. What *Dirks* proscribes is not merely a breach of confidentiality by the insider, but rather the breach of a fiduciary duty of loyalty to refrain from profiting on information entrusted to the tipper. Looking at objective criteria, courts must determine whether the insider-tipper personally benefited, directly or indirectly, from his disclosure. Secrist tipped off Dirks in order to bring Equity Funding's misconduct to light, not for any personal gain. Absent the requisite personal benefit, liability could not be imposed.

The Disclose or Abstain Rule Today

Taken together, *Chiarella* and *Dirks* replaced the *Texas Gulf Sulphur* insider trading regime with a much narrower one. Consider the following string of hypotheticals, which is loosely based on the facts of *Texas Gulf Sulphur* itself:

1. Anna Abel is a geologist working for Acme Mining Company. In the course of her work, Anna discovers a substantial ore deposit. Before informing her bosses of the discovery, Anna buys 10,000 shares of Acme stock.

2. Barry Baker is Acme's CEO. Barry informs Acme's outside counsel, Carla Charles, about the discovery and asks her to work on legal issues relating to it. Carla buys 1,000 shares of Acme stock.

3. David Delta is Acme's chief geologist. As a going away present for his daughter Donna, who is leaving home for college, David tells her about the ore discovery. Donna buys 100 Acme shares.

4. A few days later David goes out for after work drinks with a close friend, Eddie Eagle. David has a few too many adult beverages and, in the course of his drunken ramblings, starts talking about the company's ore strike. Eddie, who is unaffiliated with Acme, buys 10,000 Acme shares.

5. As a result of all the trading, tipping, and leaking that has been going on, rumors begin to spread throughout the mining industry that "something big" is up at Acme. Although they remain uncertain whether the rumors have any validity, the directors of Ajax Mining Company decide that the time is ripe to make a long-planned hostile takeover bid for Acme. Ajax therefore begins quietly buying Acme stock, eventually acquiring over 100,000 shares.

6. Ajax's board of directors instructs its outside legal counsel, Gilda Gekko, to begin working on the legal documentation necessary for Ajax's bid. Before doing so, Gilda buys 200 Acme shares.

In each of these cases, those who traded did so while in possession of nonpublic information. In cases 1–4, the trader acted on "inside information." In cases 5 and 6, the traders acted on market information. (Assume the information was material in all cases.)

Under *Texas Gulf Sulphur*, liability could be imposed at least in cases 1–4 and 6. In each, the trader had access to information unavailable to other market participants. Only case 5 presents any difficulty. While an expansive reading of *Texas Gulf Sulphur* could justify liability here, Ajax is acting on the basis of information about its *own* intentions. It is unlikely that any court would have interpreted *Texas Gulf Sulphur* as requiring liability in such a case. How would these cases come out under the *Chiarella/Dirks* framework?

The Requisite Fiduciary Relationship and the Class of Potential Defendants

At the outset, we need to deal with a serious conceptual problem: Post-*Chiarella* and *Dirks*, liability for insider trading can be imposed only on persons who owe fiduciary duties to those with whom they trade: agents, fiduciaries, persons in whom the investors had placed their trust and confidence. Unfortunately, in neither case did the Supreme Court do a very good job of fleshing out this requirement. Is it enough that a fiduciary relationship exist, without any breach of the duties arising out of it? If a breach is required, which duty must be breached? What law determines whether the requisite fiduciary relationship and/or breach of duty is present in a particular fact pattern? Under state law, for example, corporate officers and directors generally owe no fiduciary duty to bondholders. Can insiders therefore inside trade in debt securities with impunity? Although corporate officers and directors owe fiduciary duties to their shareholders, we've seen that in many states insider trading does not breach those duties. Can insiders of firms incorporated in those states inside trade with impunity?

Defining the Fiduciary Duty Requirement. In both *Chiarella* and *Dirks*, the Supreme Court frequently spoke of the need to show the existence of a "fiduciary relationship" as a predicate to liability.[60] It left unclear, however, whether the government also must prove a breach of a duty arising out of that relationship. One passage from Justice Powell's *Dirks* opinion suggests that breach of duty is an element of the insider trading cause of action, but at the same time implied that the requisite breach will be found whenever a fiduciary trades on inside information:

60. E.g., *Dirks v. SEC*, 463 U.S. 646, 654 (1983); *Chiarella v. United States*, 445 U.S. 222, 232 (1980).

> In the seminal case of *In re Cady, Roberts & Co.*, the SEC recognized that the common law in some jurisdictions imposes on "corporate 'insiders,' particularly officers, directors, or controlling shareholders" an "affirmative duty of disclosure ... when dealing in securities." The SEC found that ... breach of this common law duty also establish[ed] the elements of a Rule 10b–5 violation....[61]

Unfortunately, while Justice Powell's opinion acknowledged that this common-law duty exists only in "some jurisdictions," he went on—without any explanation or citation of authority—to extrapolate therefrom a rule that all "insiders [are] forbidden by their fiduciary relationship from personally using undisclosed corporate information to their advantage." Given that such a rule exists only in "some jurisdictions," the requisite fiduciary obligation apparently arises out of federal—not state—law. A federal source for the fiduciary relationship element also is suggested by Justice Powell's contention "that '[a] significant purpose of the Exchange Act was to eliminate the idea that use of inside information for personal advantage was a normal emolument of corporate office.' " His repeated references to a "*Cady, Roberts* duty" may also point towards a federal source for the requisite duty. There is at least the implication that *Cady, Roberts* created a federal duty prohibiting insider trading, which has become part of the overall bundle of fiduciary duties to which insiders are subject.

61. *Dirks*, 463 U.S. at 653.

This understanding of *Dirks* was implicitly confirmed by the Supreme Court's more recent decision in *United States v. O'Hagan*.[62] The majority reaffirmed the *Chiarella/Dirks* requirement of a fiduciary relationship, broadly holding that the "relationship of trust and confidence" between insiders and shareholders "gives rise to a duty to disclose" or to abstain. Again, given that many states impose no such duty on corporate officers and directors, one must assume that the duty of which the court spoke is federal in origin.

Accordingly, in applying the modern disclose or abstain rule, one must first determine whether a fiduciary relationship exists between the inside trader and those with whom he is about to trade. Presumably one looks to federal law to make that determination, although we shall see that this proves quite problematic. If the requisite fiduciary relationship is present, the disclose or abstain obligation attaches.

The trouble is that the *Dirks/O'Hagan* framework makes no logical sense and, worse yet, is inconsistent with the Supreme Court's Rule 10b–5 jurisprudence. In the first place, merely showing a fiduciary relationship between the inside trader and those with whom he trades should not be enough. As Justice Frankfurter put it, albeit in a different context, "to say that a man is a fiduciary only

62. 521 U.S. 642 (1997). Although *O'Hagan* arose under the so-called misappropriation theory, rather than the disclose or abstain rule, this aspect of the opinion appears to be of general applicability.

begins analysis; it gives direction to further inquiry. To whom is he a fiduciary? What obligations does he owe as a fiduciary? In what respect has he failed to discharge those obligations?"[63] Before insider trading liability can be imposed, the government should be required to prove the defendant violated a fiduciary duty arising out of the fiduciary relationship in question. This conclusion seemingly is confirmed by the Supreme Court's treatment of tippee liability. Recall that under *Dirks*, it is not enough to show that the tipper was party to a fiduciary relationship with the source of the information. There must also be a breach of the tipper's fiduciary duty before tippee liability can result.

Assuming a breach of fiduciary duty is required, which is the duty whose violation triggers insider trading liability? As Justice Frankfurter's comment suggests, any given fiduciary relationship carries with it a number of obligations. The nature of those obligations, moreover, varies from one type of fiduciary relationship to another. A corporate director may enter into various types of contracts with the corporation, for example, that would be barred in the case of a trustee dealing with trust assets. Unfortunately, the Supreme Court once again was not very precise on this score. Its opinions speak mainly of a duty to disclose before trading, but left the issue uncertain.

Some lower courts phrased the inquiry in terms of a duty of confidentiality—asking whether the inside trader had violated a duty to keep the infor-

63. *SEC v. Chenery Corp.*, 318 U.S. 80, 85–86 (1943).

mation in question confidential.[64] Using a duty of
confidentiality as the requisite fiduciary duty, however, makes little sense in the insider trading context. Unlike most types of tangible property, the
same piece of information can be used by more than
one person at the same time; an insider's use of the
information, moreover, does not necessarily lower
its value to its owner. When an executive that has
just negotiated a major contract for his employer
thereafter inside trades in the employer's stock, for
example, the value of the contract to the employer
has not been lowered nor, absent some act of disclosure, has the executive violated his duty of confidentiality. Using nonpublic information for personal
gain thus is not inconsistent with a duty of confidentiality, unless one's trades somehow reveal the
information.

The only coherent approach is to hold that the
fiduciary duty requirement requires a breach by the
inside trader of a duty to refrain from self-dealing
in nonpublic information. This conclusion finds
some support in *Dirks*. Justice Powell, for example,
described the elements of an insider trading violation as: "(i) the existence of a relationship affording
access to inside information intended to be available
only for a corporate purpose, and (ii) the unfairness
of allowing a corporate insider to take advantage of
that information by trading without disclosure."
Another passage likewise described insider trading

64. See, e.g., *United States v. Libera*, 989 F.2d 596 (2d
Cir.1993), cert. denied, 510 U.S. 976 (1993); *United States v.
Carpenter*, 791 F.2d 1024, 1034 (2d Cir.1986), aff'd on other
grounds, 484 U.S. 19 (1987).

liability as arising from "the 'inherent unfairness involved where one takes advantage' of 'information intended to be available only for a corporate purpose and not for the personal benefit of anyone.' " Yet another noted that insiders are "forbidden by their fiduciary relationship from using undisclosed corporate information for their personal gain." The focus in each instance is on the duty to refrain from self-dealing.

The Santa Fe Problem. Recall that in *Santa Fe Industries, Inc. v. Green*,[65] the Supreme Court held that Rule 10b–5 is concerned with disclosure and fraud, not with fiduciary duties. The court did so in large measure out of a concern that the contrary decision would result in federalizing much of state corporate law and thereby overriding well-established state policies of corporate regulation. While its holding is not squarely on point, the rationale of *Santa Fe* seems directly applicable to the insider trading prohibition. The court held, for example, that Rule 10b–5 did not reach claims "in which the essence of the complaint is that shareholders were treated unfairly by a fiduciary." This is of course the very essence of the complaint made in insider trading cases. The court also held that extension of Rule 10b–5 to breaches of fiduciary duty was unjustified in light of the state law remedies available to plaintiffs. As we have seen, insider trading plaintiffs likewise have state law remedies available to them. Granted, those remedies vary from state to state and are likely to prove unavailing in many

65. 430 U.S. 462 (1977).

cases, but the same was true of the state law appraisal remedy at issue in *Santa Fe*. Finally, the court expressed reluctance "to federalize the substantial portion of the law of corporations that deals with transactions in securities, particularly where established state policies of corporate regulation would be overridden." In view of the state law standards discussed above, of course, this is precisely what the federal insider trading prohibition did. Given that *Santa Fe* requires that all other corporate fiduciary duties be left to state law, why should insider trading be singled out for special treatment?

Dirks and *Chiarella* simply ignored the doctrinal tension between their fiduciary duty-based regime and *Santa Fe*. In *O'Hagan*, Justice Ginsburg's majority opinion at least recognized that *Santa Fe* presented a problem for the federal insider trading prohibition, but her purported solution is quite unconvincing. Justice Ginsburg correctly described *Santa Fe* as "underscoring that § 10(b) is not an all-purpose breach of fiduciary duty ban; rather it trains on conduct involving manipulation or deception."[66] Instead of acknowledging that insider trading is mainly a fiduciary duty issue, however, she treated it as solely a disclosure issue. It is thus the failure to disclose that one is about to inside trade that is the problem, not the trade itself: "A fiduciary who '[pretends] loyalty to the principal while secretly converting the principal's information for personal gain' ... 'dupes' or defrauds the principal." As Justice Ginsburg acknowledged, this ap-

66. *U.S. v. O'Hagan*, 117 S. Ct. 2199, 2209 (1997).

proach means that full disclosure must preclude liability. If the prospective inside trader informs the persons with whom he or she is about to trade that "he plans to trade on the nonpublic information, there is no 'deceptive device' and thus no § 10(b) liability...."

Justice Ginsburg's approach fails to solve the problem. Granted, insider trading involves deception in the sense that the defendant by definition failed to disclose nonpublic information before trading. Persons subject to the disclose or abstain theory, however, often are also subject to a state law-based fiduciary duty of confidentiality, which precludes them from disclosing the information. As to them, the insider trading prohibition collapses into a requirement to abstain from trading on material nonpublic information. As such, it really is their failure to abstain from trading, rather than their nondisclosure, which is the basis for imposing liability. A former SEC Commissioner more or less admitted as much: "Unlike much securities regulation, the insider trading rules probably do not result in more information coming into the market: The 'abstain or disclose' rule for those entrusted with confidential information usually is observed by abstention."[67] Yet, *Santa Fe* clearly precludes the creation of such duties.

In any event, Justice Ginsburg's solution also is essentially circular. Recall that failure to disclose material nonpublic information before trading does

67. Charles C. Cox & Kevin S. Fogarty, *Bases of Insider Trading Law*, 49 Ohio St. L.J. 353 (1988).

not always violate Rule 10b–5. In omission cases, which include all insider trading on impersonal stock exchanges, liability can be imposed only if the defendant had a duty to disclose before trading. If Rule 10b–5 itself creates the requisite duty, however, this requirement is effectively negated. As such, the requisite duty must come from outside the securities laws. Indeed, given *Santa Fe*, it must come from outside federal law. Yet, as we have seen, the *Dirks/O'Hagan* framework appears to violate this requirement through circularity—creating a federal disclosure obligation arising out of Rule 10b–5.

Bottom line? The conceptual conflict between the Supreme Court's current insider trading jurisprudence and its more general Rule 10b–5 precedents remains unresolved.[68] It seems reasonably clear that the principal task is to determine whether a fiduciary relationship exists between the inside trader and the person with whom he or she trades. Whether that determination is made as a matter of state or federal law, unfortunately, is unclear. *O'Hagan* confirms that the attorney-client relationship is a fiduciary one. Dictum in all three Supreme Court precedents tells us that corporate officers and directors are fiduciaries of their shareholders. Beyond these two categories we must make educated guesses. The

68. See generally Stephen M. Bainbridge, *Incorporating State Law Fiduciary Duties into the Federal Insider Trading Prohibition*, 52 Wash. & Lee L. Rev. 1189 (1995); Richard W. Painter et al., *Don't Ask, Just Tell: Insider Trading after* United States v. O'Hagan, 84 Va. L. Rev. 153 (1998); Larry E. Ribstein, *Federalism and Insider Trading*, 6 Sup. Ct Econ. Rev. 123 (1998).

sections that follow use the hypotheticals recounted earlier to provide as much guidance on this issue as possible. Until a majority of the Supreme Court has held that a particular relationship is fiduciary in nature, however, we cannot know for sure.

Insiders. At common law, the insider trading prohibition focused on corporate officers and directors. As Chapter 5 explains, the short-swing profit insider trading restrictions provided by § 16(b) similarly are likewise limited to officers, directors, and shareholders owning more than 10 percent of the company's stock. One of the many issues first addressed in the seminal *Texas Gulf Sulphur* case was whether § 10(b) was restricted to that class of persons. Some of the *Texas Gulf Sulphur* defendants were middle managers and field workers. The *Texas Gulf Sulphur* court had little difficulty finding that such mid-level corporate employees were insiders for purposes of Rule 10b–5. But that holding followed directly from the court's equal access test: "Insiders, as directors or management officers are, of course, by this Rule, precluded from [insider] dealing, but the Rule is also applicable to one possessing [nonpublic] information who may not be strictly termed an 'insider' within the meaning of [section] 16(b) of the Act."[69] *Chiarella*'s rejection of the equal access test thus reopened the question of how far down the corporate ladder Rule 10b–5 extended.

69. *SEC v. Texas Gulf Sulphur Co.*, 401 F.2d 833, 848 (2d Cir.), cert. denied, 394 U.S. 976 (1969).

Recall that the Supreme Court had said Chiarella could not be held liable under Rule 10b–5 because, as to the target companies' shareholders, "he was not their agent, he was not a fiduciary, [and] he was not a person in whom the sellers had placed their trust and confidence."[70] In our hypotheticals, it cannot be said that Anna Abel (the Acme geologist who discovered the ore deposit) is a person in whom Acme's shareholders have placed their trust and confidence—after all, Acme's shareholders likely do not even know of Anna's existence. On the other hand, Anna is an agent of Acme and, as such, likely will be deemed a fiduciary of Acme's shareholders for purposes of Rule 10b–5. Although the question of whether all corporate employees will be deemed insiders remains open, there seems little doubt that the insider trading prohibition includes not only directors and officers, but also at least those key employees who have been given access to confidential information for corporate purposes. In *Chiarella*, the majority opinion implied that the duty to disclose or abstain applies to anyone in "a relationship [with the issuer] affording access to inside information intended to be available only for corporate purpose." The Second Circuit likewise has stated that: "it is well settled the traditional corporate 'insiders'—directors, officers and persons who have access to confidential information—must preserve the confidentiality of nonpublic information that belongs to and emanates from the corporation."[71]

70. *Chiarella v. United States*, 445 U.S. 222, 232 (1980).

71. *Moss v. Morgan Stanley Inc.*, 719 F.2d 5, 10 (2d Cir. 1983), cert. denied, 465 U.S. 1025 (1984).

Anna Abel, Barry Baker, and David Delta are all captured by this formulation. Anna presumably is a key employee, charged with developing precisely this sort of information for the corporation. David (Anna's supervisor) also is a key employee, who presumably is given access to the information so that he can do his job. As Acme's CEO, Barry is an insider simply by virtue of being an officer of the corporation.

Suppose, however, that Anna had written a memo to her supervisors describing the ore discovery. A janitorial employee of Acme's discovered the memo while cleaning Anna's office and bought a few shares. Although the janitor may be an agent of Acme, he is not a key employee given access to confidential information for a corporate purpose. It is therefore doubtful whether he should be regarded as an insider for Rule 10b–5 purposes.

None of the other characters in our hypotheticals are insiders. Gilda Gekko's position as Ajax's (the prospective acquirer) counsel is directly analogous to Chiarella's position as a printer for acquiring companies—as to the target companies' shareholders, both are outsiders and strangers. Ajax itself is an outsider and, moreover, is trading on the basis of its own intentions. Because *Chairella* premised liability on misuse of information entrusted to the trader by another, trading on the basis of one's own intentions is not actionable under Rule 10b–5. Eddie and Donna (respectively the friend and daughter of David Delta) both have relationships with insiders, which poses potential tipping issues, but neither fairly can be described as a classic insider. Because the information was not entrusted to them for a corporate purpose, no liability can ensue under the classic disclose or abstain theory.

Constructive Insiders. Consider Carla Charles, the star of hypothetical #2. As Acme's outside legal counsel, she was informed of the ore discovery by Acme's CEO. Although Carla owes fiduciary duties to Acme by virtue of the lawyer-client relationship, she is not a classic insider. She is more akin to an independent contractor than an employee. Nevertheless, the Supreme Court has made clear that she can be treated as though she were an insider:

> Under certain circumstances, such as where corporate information is revealed legitimately to an underwriter, accountant, lawyer, or consultant working for the corporation, these outsiders may become fiduciaries of the shareholders. The basis for recognizing this fiduciary duty is not simply that such persons acquired nonpublic corporate information, but rather that they have entered into a special confidential relationship in the conduct of the business of the enterprise and are given access to information solely for corporate purposes.... For such a duty to be imposed, however, the corporation must expect the outsider to keep the disclosed nonpublic information confidential, and the relationship at least must imply such a duty.[72]

72. *Dirks v. SEC*, 463 U.S. 646, 655 n. 14 (1983).

Under this formulation, Carla Charles is a so-called constructive insider. She entered into a confidential relationship with Acme—specifically, a lawyer-client relationship—in the course of the company's business. She was given access to information about the ore strike for a corporate purpose—to work on legal issues relating to the discovery. Even in the absence of any explicit expectation of confidentiality on the corporation's part, courts dealing with inside trading by lawyers in such cases typically have inferred both the requisite expectation and the duty to respect it.

Although Donna Delta and Eddie Eagle also learned of the ore strike from corporate sources, neither will be deemed constructive insiders. Neither entered into a confidential relationship with Acme. For an outsider to be treated as a constructive insider, moreover, there must be both an affirmative expectation that the information will be used solely for the benefit of the issuer, and some sort of assent to that duty by the recipient of the information. Neither Donna nor Eddie agreed to respect the confidentiality of the information; nor did either have any sort of relationship with Acme from which such an agreement might be implied.

Although *Dirks* clearly requires that the recipient of the information in some way agree to keep it confidential, courts have sometimes overlooked that requirement. In *SEC v. Lund*,[73] for example, Lund

73. 570 F.Supp. 1397 (C.D.Cal.1983). Even under *Lund*, neither Donna nor Eddie should have liability. Unlike *Lund*, neither of our hypotheticals involved disclosures made in the course of

and another businessman discussed a proposed joint venture between their respective companies. In those discussions, Lund received confidential information about the other's firm. Lund thereafter bought stock in the other's company. The court determined that by virtue of their close personal and professional relationship, and because of the business context of the discussion, Lund was a constructive insider of the issuer. In doing so, however, the court focused almost solely on the issuer's expectation of confidentiality. It failed to inquire into whether Lund had agreed to keep the information confidential.

Lund is usefully contrasted with *Walton v. Morgan Stanley & Co.*[74] Morgan Stanley represented a company considering acquiring Olinkraft Corporation in a friendly merger. During exploratory negotiations Olinkraft gave Morgan confidential information. Morgan's client ultimately decided not to pursue the merger, but Morgan allegedly later passed the acquired information to another client planning a tender offer for Olinkraft. In addition, Morgan's arbitrage department made purchases of Olinkraft stock for its own account. The Second Circuit held that Morgan was not a fiduciary of Olinkraft: "Put bluntly, although, according to the complaint, Olinkraft's management placed its confidence in Morgan Stanley not to disclose the information, Morgan owed no duty to observe that confi-

business negotiations. Both involved purely personal relationships.

74.   623 F.2d 796 (2d Cir.1980).

dence." Although *Walton* was decided under state law, it has been cited approvingly in a number of federal insider trading opinions and is generally regarded as a more accurate statement of the law than *Lund*.[75] Indeed, a subsequent case from the same district court as *Lund* essentially acknowledged that it had been wrongly decided:

> What the Court seems to be saying in *Lund* is that anytime a person is given information by an issuer with an expectation of confidentiality or limited use, he becomes an insider of the issuer. But under *Dirks*, that is not enough; the individual must have expressly or impliedly entered into a fiduciary relationship with the issuer.[76]

Even this statement does not go far enough, however, because it does not acknowledge the additional requirement of an affirmative assumption of the duty of confidentiality.

Tippers and Tippees. Hypothetical #3 is a classic tipping case: David Delta (an insider) tells his daughter (an outsider) who then trades. David is the tipper; daughter Donna is the tippee. Recall that *Dirks* held that tippees could be held liable, provided two conditions are met: (1) the tipper breached a fiduciary duty to the corporation by making the tip and (2) the tippee knew or had reason to know of the breach.

75. See, e.g., *Dirks v. SEC*, 463 U.S. 646, 662 n. 22 (1983); *United States v. Chestman*, 947 F.2d 551, 567–58 (2d Cir.1991), cert. denied, 503 U.S. 1004 (1992); *Moss v. Morgan Stanley Inc.*, 719 F.2d 5 (2d Cir.1983), cert. denied, 465 U.S. 1025 (1984).

76. *SEC v. Ingram*, 694 F.Supp. 1437, 1440 (C.D.Cal.1988).

The requirement that the tip constitute a breach of duty on the tipper's part eliminates many cases in which an insider discloses information to an outsider. In hypothetical #2, for example, Acme's CEO told its outside legal counsel about the ore discovery. But this is not an illegal tip—no fiduciary obligation is violated by making disclosures for a legitimate corporate purpose.

Indeed, not every disclosure made in violation of a fiduciary duty constitutes an illegal tip. In hypothetical #4, for example, David may have been careless in getting drunk, but in the absence of evidence that his claimed drunkenness was a sham intended to evade the tipping rules, he at worst is guilty of violating his duty of care. What *Dirks* proscribes is not just a breach of duty, however, but a breach of the duty of loyalty forbidding fiduciaries to personally benefit from the disclosure.

An instructive case is *SEC v. Switzer*,[77] which involved Barry Switzer, the well-known former coach of the Oklahoma Sooners and Dallas Cowboys football teams. Phoenix Resources Company was an oil and gas company. One fine day in 1981, Phoenix's CEO, one George Platt, and his wife attended a track meet to watch their son compete. Coach Switzer was also at the meet, watching his son. Platt and Switzer had known each other for some time. Platt had Oklahoma season tickets and his company had sponsored Switzer's television show. Sometime in the afternoon Switzer laid down on a row of bleachers behind the Platts to sunbathe.

77.   590 F.Supp. 756 (W.D.Okla.1984).

Platt, purportedly unaware of Switzer's presence, began telling his wife about a recent business trip to New York. In that conversation, Platt mentioned his desire to dispose of or liquidate Phoenix. Platt further talked about several companies bidding on Phoenix. Platt also mentioned that an announcement of a "possible" liquidation of Phoenix might occur the following Thursday. Switzer overheard this conversation and shortly thereafter bought a substantial number of Phoenix shares and tipped off a number of his friends. Because Switzer was neither an insider or constructive insider (do you see why?) of Phoenix, the main issue was whether Platt had illegally tipped Switzer.

Per *Dirks*, the initial issue was whether Platt had violated his fiduciary duty by obtaining an improper personal benefit: "Absent some personal gain, there has been no breach of duty to stockholders. And absent a breach by the insider [to his stockholders], there is no derivative breach [by the tippee]." The court found that Platt did not obtain any improper benefit. The court further found that the information was inadvertently (and unbeknownst to Platt) overheard by Switzer. Chatting about business with one's spouse in a public place may be careless, but it is not a breach of one's duty of loyalty.

The next issue is whether Switzer knew or should have known of the breach. Given that there was no breach by Platt, of course, this prong of the *Dirks* test by definition could not be met. But it is instructive that the court went on to explicitly hold that

"Rule 10b–5 does not bar trading on the basis of information inadvertently revealed by an insider."

Eddie Eagle (the friend of the drunken insider) will argue that his position is analogous to Switzer's. David Delta did not intentionally disclose the information; nor did he do so for personal gain. Instead, he inadvertently disclosed it while rambling drunkenly. A legally sound argument, although query whether the jury is likely to believe it. In *Switzer*, which was tried in Oklahoma, the court simply did not believe the SEC's allegation that Platt intended to pass the information to Switzer.

In hypothetical #3, Donna Delta might try to argue that her father did not personally gain from the tip, but this argument would be unavailing. In *Dirks*, the Supreme Court identified several situations in which the requisite personal benefit can be found. The most obvious is the quid pro quo setting, in which the tipper gets some form of pecuniary gain. Nonpecuniary gain can also qualify, however. Suppose a corporate CEO discloses information to a wealthy investor not for any legitimate corporate purpose, but solely to enhance his own reputation. *Dirks* would find a personal benefit on those facts. Finally, and most relevantly to our hypothetical, *Dirks* indicated that liability could be imposed where the tip is a gift. David's gift to Donna satisfies the breach element because it is analogous to the situation in which David trades on the basis of the information and then gives his daughter the profits.

Some concluding observations about the *Dirks* tipping formulation: Note that, at least in theory, it is possible for a tipper to be liable even if the tippee is not liable. The breach of duty is enough to render the tipper liable, but the tippee must know of the breach in order to be held liable. Notice also that it is possible to have chains of tipping liability: Tipper tells Tippee #1 who tells Tippee #2 who trades. Tippee #2 can be held liable, so long as she knew or had reason to know that the ultimate source of the information had breached his fiduciary duties by disclosing it.

Nontraditional Relationships. Once we get outside the traditional categories of Rule 10b–5 defendants—insiders, constructive insiders, and their tippees—things get much more complicated. Suppose a doctor learned confidential information from a patient, upon which she then traded? Is she an insider? As the Second Circuit cogently observed in *United States v. Chestman*:

[F]iduciary duties are circumscribed with some clarity in the context of shareholder relations but lack definition in other contexts. Tethered to the field of shareholder relations, fiduciary obligations arise within a narrow, principled sphere. The existence of fiduciary duties in other common law settings, however, is anything but clear. Our Rule 10b–5 precedents ..., moreover, provide little guidance with respect to the question of fiduciary breach, because they involved egregious fiduciary breaches arising solely in the context of employer/employee associations.[78]

The best guidance to date on this issue in fact remains the *Chestman* decision. Ira Waldbaum was the president and controlling shareholder of Waldbaum, Inc., a publicly-traded supermarket chain. Ira decided to sell Waldbaum to A & P at $50 per share, a 100% premium over the prevailing market price. Ira informed his sister Shirley of the forthcoming transaction. Shirley told her daughter Susan Loeb, who in turn told her husband Keith Loeb. Each person in the chain told the next to keep the information confidential. Keith passed an edited version of the information to his stockbroker, one Robert Chestman, who then bought Waldbaum stock for his own account and the accounts of other clients. Chestman was accused of violating Rule 10b–5. According to the Government's theory of the case, Keith Loeb owed fiduciary duties to his wife Susan, which he violated by trading and tipping Chestman.

The Second Circuit held that in the absence of any evidence that Keith regularly participated in confidential business discussions, the familial relationship standing alone did not create a fiduciary relationship between Keith and Susan or any members of her family. Accordingly, Loeb's actions did

78.   947 F.2d 551, 567 (2d Cir.1991) (citations omitted), cert. denied 503 U.S. 1004 (1992). *Chestman* was a misappropriation theory case, as have been most of the nontraditional relationship cases. The problem it addressed and the principles announced therein, however, are applicable to insider trading cases generally. Accordingly, it seems appropriate to treat this issue here.

not give rise to the requisite breach of fiduciary duty.

In reaching that conclusion, the court laid out a general framework for dealing with nontraditional relationships. The court began by identifying two factors that did not by themselves justify finding a fiduciary relationship between Keith and Susan. First, unilaterally entrusting someone with confidential information does not by itself create a fiduciary relationship.[79] This is true even if the disclosure is accompanied by an admonition such as "don't tell," which Susan's statements to Keith included. Second, familial relationships are not fiduciary in nature without some additional element.

Turning to factors that could justify finding a fiduciary relationship on these facts, the court first identified a list of "inherently fiduciary" associations:

> Counted among these hornbook fiduciary relations are those existing between attorney and client, executor and heir, guardian and ward, principal and agent, trustee and trust beneficiary, and senior corporate official and shareholder. While this list is by no means exhaustive, it is clear that the relationships involved in this case— those between Keith and Susan Loeb and be-

79. Repeated disclosures of business secrets, however, could substitute for a factual finding of dependence and influence and, accordingly, sustain a finding that a fiduciary relationship existed in the case at bar. *Chestman*, 947 F.2d at 569. Hence, the court's emphasis on the absence of such repeated disclosures as between Keith and Susan or her family.

tween Keith Loeb and the Waldbaum family—
were not traditional fiduciary relationships.

In our hypotheticals, for example, Gilda Gekko, by
virtue of her position as outside legal counsel for
the potential acquirer, would be deemed a fiduciary
for purposes of Rule 10b–5, albeit of Ajax—not
Acme. Although Gilda cannot be prosecuted under
the classic disclose or abstain theory, her status as a
fiduciary makes her vulnerable to prosecution under the misappropriation theory, which is discussed
below.

A rather serious problem with the *Chestman*
court's glib assertion that the specified relationships are "inherently fiduciary" is the resulting
failure to seriously evaluate whether any duty arising out of such relationships was violated by the
defendant's conduct. In *United States v. Willis*,[80] for
example, the court determined that a psychiatrist
violated the prohibition by trading on information
learned from a patient. In determining that the
requisite breach of fiduciary duty had occurred, the
court relied in large measure on the Hippocratic
Oath. In relevant part, the Oath reads: "Whatsoev-
er things I see or hear concerning the life of men, in
my attendance on the sick or even apart therefrom,
which ought not to be noised abroad, I will keep
silence thereon, counting such things to be as sa-
cred secrets." While the Oath thus imposes a duty
of confidentiality on those who take it, it does not
forbid them from self-dealing in information
learned from patients so long as the information is

80.   737 F.Supp. 269 (S.D.N.Y.1990).

not thereby disclosed. As such, it is not at all clear
that the requisite breach of duty was present in
Willis. Unfortunately, as *Willis* illustrates, these
issues routinely are swept under the rug.

In any event, once one moves beyond the class of
"hornbook" fiduciary relationships,[81] *Chestman*
held that the requisite relationship will be found
where one party acts on the other's behalf and
"great trust and confidence" exists between the
parties:

A fiduciary relationship involves discretionary authority and dependency: One person depends on
another—the fiduciary—to serve his interests. In

81. In *Chestman*, the court observed that the requisite relationship could be satisfied either by a fiduciary relationship or a
"similar relationship of trust and confidence." 947 F.2d at 568.
So expanding the class of relationships that can give rise to
liability may lead to a results-oriented approach. If a court
wishes to impose liability, it need simply conclude that the
relationship in question involves trust and confidence, even
though the relationship bears no resemblance to those in which
fiduciary-like duties are normally imposed. Accordingly, courts
should be loath to use this phraseology as a mechanism for
expanding the scope of liability. The *Chestman* court was sensitive to this possibility, holding that a relationship of trust and
confidence must be "the functional equivalent of a fiduciary
relationship" before liability can be imposed. *Chestman* also
indicates that regardless of which type of relationship is present
the defendant must be shown to have been subject to a duty
(incorrectly described by the court as one of confidentiality) and
to have breached that duty. Finally, the court indicated that at
least as to criminal cases, it would not expand the class of
relationships from which liability might arise to encompass those
outside the traditional core of fiduciary obligation. Accordingly,
for most purposes it should be safe to disregard any possible
distinction between fiduciary relationships and other relationships of "trust and confidence."

relying on a fiduciary to act for his benefit, the beneficiary of the relation may entrust the fiduciary with custody over property of one sort or another. Because the fiduciary obtains access to this property to serve the ends of the fiduciary relationship, he becomes duty-bound not to appropriate the property for his own use.

In the insider trading context, of course, the relevant property is confidential information belonging to the principal. Because the relationship between Keith and Susan did not involve either discretionary authority or dependency of this sort, their relationship was not fiduciary in character.

The *Chestman* framework is yet another area in which the federalism concerns raised by *Santa Fe* ought to have figured more prominently than they did. As we have seen, the requisite fiduciary duty cannot be derived from Rule 10b–5 itself without making the rule incoherently circular and, moreover, violating *Santa Fe*. Unfortunately, the *Chestman* court simply ignored this problem. The court created a generic framework for deciding whether a fiduciary relationship is present, which purports to take its "cues as to what is required to create the requisite relationship from the securities fraud precedents and the common law." The court thus mixed both federal and state law sources without much regard either for potential circularity or federalism.

Other Elements

It is not enough merely to show that the alleged inside trader falls into one of the proper classes of potential defendants, of course. The insider trading cause of action includes a number of other elements, among which the most important are: (1) the information must be material; (2) the information must be nonpublic; (3) the defendant must have traded while in possession of such information or, perhaps, on the basis of such information. It may also be the case that the defendant must have traded in equity securities, as it is not clear whether trading in debt securities violates the federal insider trading prohibition.

The general Rule 10b–5 materiality standards discussed in Chapter 2 apply in full force to the insider trading prohibition. This section examines the remaining unique elements of the prohibition in turn.

Nonpublic Information; or When Can Insiders Trade? In most cases, as we have seen, the disclose or abstain rule collapses into a duty of abstention—disclosure typically is not a feasible alternative, as there usually is a legitimate corporate purpose for keeping the nonpublic information confidential. How long does this abstention obligation run? When can insiders start trading in their company's securities?

The simple answer is that insiders may only trade after the information in question has been made public. The difficulty, of course, is knowing whether or not the information in question has entered the public domain. Because insiders with access to confidential information trade at their own risk, this timing issue is a critical question.

Texas Gulf Sulphur again is instructive. The ore strike was first announced by a press release to the Canadian news media disseminated at 9:40 a.m. on April 16, 1964. A news conference with the American media followed at 10 a.m. on the same day. The news appeared on the Dow Jones ticker tape at 10:54 a.m. that day. Defendant Crawford had telephoned his stockbroker at midnight on the 15th with instructions to buy TGS stock when the Midwest Stock Exchange opened the next morning. Defendant Coates left the April 16th news conference to call his stockbroker shortly before 10:20 a.m. In addition to executing Coates' order, the broker ordered an additional 1500 TGS shares for himself and other customers. Crawford and Coates conceded that they traded while in possession of material information, but claimed that the information had been effectively disseminated to the public (and thus had lost its nonpublic character) before their trades were executed.

The court disagreed, holding that before insiders may act upon material information, the information must have been disclosed in a manner that ensures its availability to the investing public. Merely waiting until a press release has been read to reporters, as Coates did, is not enough. The information must have been widely disseminated and public investors must have an opportunity to act on it. At a minimum, the court opined, insiders therefore must wait until the news could reasonably be expected to appear over the Dow Jones ticker tape—the news service that transmits investment news to brokers and investment professionals.

Unlike other aspects of *Texas Gulf Sulphur*, this rule is still good law today. It also makes good policy sense. The efficient capital markets hypothesis, about which more will be said in Chapter 4, tells us that all currently available public information about a corporation is reflected in the market price of its securities. However, the hypothesis depends on the ability of investment professionals to adjust their selling and offering prices to reflect that information. By requiring that insiders wait until the news has gone out over the Dow Jones wire, the court assured that brokers would have the information before trading; in other words, the price should have already started rising (or falling, as the case may be) to reflect the new information.

While the *Texas Gulf Sulphur* standard works well for the sort of dramatic, one-time event news at issue there, it works less well for the more mundane sorts of nonpublic information to which insiders routinely have access. A corporation always has undisclosed information about numerous different aspects of its business. By the time all of that information has been disseminated publicly, moreover, new undisclosed information doubtless will have been developed. In response to this concern, many firms have developed policies pursuant to which insiders may only trade during a specified window of time after the corporation has issued its quarterly and annual reports. Per SEC regulations, public corporations must send an annual report to the shareholders and also file a Form 10–Q after each of the first three quarters of their fiscal year and a Form 10–K after year's end. Because of the substantial and wide-ranging disclosures required in these reports, which are publicly available, there is a relatively low probability that an insider who trades during the time immediately following their dissemination will be deemed to have traded on material nonpublic information. As *Texas Gulf Sulphur* suggests, however, the insider may not trade the moment the report goes in the mail. Instead, the insider must wait until the market has had time to digest the report. In any event, of course, an insider who knows that he or she possesses material information that was not disclosed in the report must refrain from trading at all times—whether or not the corporation has released a periodic disclosure report.

Possession v. Use. Recall the facts of *Diamond v. Oreamuno,* discussed in Chapter 2 above. Insiders of MAI sold their holdings of firm stock while in possession of bad news that was both material and nonpublic. As such, they avoided significant losses that would have resulted from the drop in MAI's stock price that occurred when the bad news was made public. Suppose one of the defendants claimed the bad news had not caused his sale—he would have sold his MAI stock regardless of whether he thought the stock would be going up or down in the future. Perhaps he needed money to pay catastrophic medical bills, for example. Alternatively, perhaps he had a pattern of disposing of MAI stock at regular intervals. Many senior corporate executives receive a substantial portion of their compensation in the form of stock grants or options, which they periodically liquidate to realize their cash value. In either case, our hypothetical defendant would have traded while in possession of material nonpublic information, but not on the basis of such information. Can he be held liable?

The SEC long has argued that trading while in knowing possession of material nonpublic information satisfies Rule 10b–5's scienter requirement. In *United States v. Teicher*,[82] the Second Circuit agreed, albeit in a passage that appears to be dictum. An attorney tipped stock market speculators about transactions involving clients of his firm. On appeal, defendants objected to a jury instruction pursuant to which they could be found guilty of securities fraud based upon the mere possession of fraudulently obtained material nonpublic information without regard to whether that information was the actual cause of their transactions. The Second Circuit held that any error in the instruction was harmless, but went on to opine in favor of a knowing possession test. The court interpreted *Chiarella* as comporting with "the oft-quoted maxim that one with a fiduciary or similar duty to hold material nonpublic information in confidence must

82.   987 F.2d 112 (2d Cir.1993).

either 'disclose or abstain' with regard to trading." The court also favored the possession standard because it "recognizes that one who trades while knowingly possessing material inside information has an informational advantage over other traders." The difficulties with the court's reasoning should be apparent. In the first place, a mere possession test is inconsistent with Rule 10b–5's scienter requirement, which requires fraudulent intent (or, at least, recklessness). In the second, contrary to the court's view, *Chiarella* simply did not address the distinction between a knowing possession and a use standard. Finally, the court's reliance on the trader's informational advantage is inconsistent with *Chiarella*'s rejection of the equal access test.

In *SEC v. Adler*,[83] the Eleventh Circuit rejected *Teicher* in favor of a use standard. Under *Adler*, "when an insider trades while in possession of material nonpublic information, a strong inference arises that such information was used by the insider in trading. The insider can attempt to rebut the inference by adducing evidence that there was no causal connection between the information and the trade—i.e., that the information was not used." Although defendant Pegram apparently possessed material nonpublic information at the time he trad-

83. 137 F.3d 1325 (11th Cir.1998). The Ninth Circuit recently agreed with *Adler* that proof of use, not mere possession, is required. The Ninth Circuit further held that in criminal cases no presumption of use should be drawn from the fact of possession—the government must affirmatively proof use of nonpublic information. *United States v. Smith*, 155 F.3d 1051 (9th Cir. 1998).

ed, he introduced strong evidence that he had a plan to sell company stock and that that plan predated his acquisition of the information in question. If proven at trial, evidence of such a pre-existing plan would rebut the inference of use and justify an acquittal on grounds that he lacked the requisite scienter. Similarly, the court opined, evidence that the allegedly illegal trades were consistent with trading also would rebut the inference of use.

The choice between *Adler* and *Teicher* is difficult. On the one hand, in adopting the Insider Trading Sanctions Act of 1984,[84] Congress imposed treble money civil fines on those who illegally trade "while in possession" of material nonpublic information. In addition, a use standard significantly complicates the government's burden in insider trading cases, because motivation is always harder to establish than possession, although the inference of use permitted by *Adler* substantially alleviates this concern. On the other hand, a number of decisions have acknowledged that a pre-existing plan and/or prior trading pattern can be introduced as an affirmative defense in insider trading cases, as such evidence tends to disprove that defendant acted with the requisite scienter. Dictum in each of the Supreme Court's insider trading opinions also appears to endorse the use standard. In light of the Circuit split that now exists between *Teicher* and *Adler*, one suspects that the Supreme Court will eventually have to resolve the conflict.

84. The Act is described in detail *infra* pages 122–23.

Trading in Debt Securities. One of the areas in which the Supreme Court's failure to specify the source and nature of the fiduciary obligation underlying the disclose or abstain rule has proven especially problematic is insider trading in debt securities. Yet, the prohibition's application to debt securities has received surprisingly little judicial attention. One court has held that insider trading in convertible debentures violates Rule 10b–5,[85] but this case is clearly distinguishable from nonconvertible debt securities. Because they are convertible into common stock at the option of the holder, both the market price and interest rate paid on such instruments are affected by the market price of the underlying common stock. Federal securities law recognizes the close relationship of convertibles to common stock by defining the former as equity securities. As such, the status of noncovertible debt remains unresolved. A strong argument can be made, however, that the prohibition should not extend to trading in nonconvertible debt.

In most states, neither the corporation nor its officers and directors have fiduciary duties to debtholders. Instead, debtholders' rights are limited to the express terms of the contract and an implied covenant of good faith.[86] Cases in a few jurisdictions purport to recognize fiduciary duties running to

85. *In re Worlds of Wonder Securities Litigation*, [1990–1991 Trans. Binder] Fed. Sec. L. Rep. (CCH) ¶ 95,689 (N.D.Cal. 1990).

86. See, e.g., *Metropolitan Life Ins. Co. v. RJR Nabisco, Inc.*, 716 F.Supp. 1504 (S.D.N.Y.1989); *Katz v. Oak Indus.*, 508 A.2d 873 (Del.Ch.1986).

holders of debt securities, but the duties imposed in these cases are more accurately characterized as the same implied covenant of good faith found in most other jurisdictions.[87]

The distinction between this implied covenant and a fiduciary duty is an important one for our purposes. An implied covenant of good faith arises from the express terms of a contract and is used to fulfill the parties' mutual intent. In contrast, a fiduciary duty has little to do with the parties' intent. Instead, courts use fiduciary duties to protect the interests of the duty's beneficiary. Accordingly, a fiduciary duty requires the party subject to the duty to put the interests of the beneficiary of the duty ahead of his own, while an implied duty of good faith merely requires both parties to respect their bargain.

A two-step move thus will be required if courts are to impose liability under the disclose or abstain rule on those who inside trade in debt securities. First, the clear holdings of *Chiarella* and *Dirks* must be set aside so that the requisite relationship can be expanded to include purely contractual arrangements and the requisite duty expanded to include mere contractual covenants. Second, the implied covenant of good faith must be interpreted as barring self-dealing in nonpublic information by corporate agents. In that regard, consider the lead-

87. See, e.g., *Broad v. Rockwell Int'l Corp.*, 642 F.2d 929 (5th Cir.), cert. denied, 454 U.S. 965 (1981); *Gardner & Florence Call Cowles Found. v. Empire, Inc.*, 589 F.Supp. 669 (S.D.N.Y.1984), vacated, 754 F.2d 478 (2d Cir.1985); *Fox v. MGM Grand Hotels, Inc.*, 187 Cal.Rptr. 141 (Cal.Ct.App.1982).

ing *Met Life* decision, which indicates that a cove-nant of good faith will be implied only when neces-sary to ensure that neither side deprives the other side of the fruits of the agreement.[88] The fruits of the agreement are limited to regular payment of interest and ultimate repayment of principal. Be-cause insider trading rarely affects either of these fruits, it does not violate the covenant of good faith.[89]

To be sure, the courts could simply ignore state law. Yet, the Supreme Court has consistently held that insider trading liability requires an agency or fiduciary relationship. As to common stock, *Dirks* created what appears to be a federal fiduciary obli-gation, but recall that that obligation was extrapo-lated from state common law. It seems unlikely that the courts will treat the state law status of debtholders as irrelevant.

Insofar as public policy is concerned, the argu-ment for creating fiduciary duties—federal or

88. *Metropolitan Life Ins. Co. v. RJR Nabisco, Inc.*, 716 F.Supp. 1504, 1517 (S.D.N.Y.1989).

89. Various alternative theories of liability may come into play in this context. In particular, the misappropriation theory might apply. Suppose a corporate officer traded in the firm's debt securities using material nonpublic information belonging to the corporation. As the argument would go, even though the officer owes no fiduciary duties to the bondholders, he owes fiduciary duties to the corporation. The violation of those duties might suffice for liability under the misappropriation theory. The mis-appropriation theory clearly would not reach trading by an issuer in its own debt securities, which would come under the disclose or abstain rule.

state—running to bondholders is extremely weak. Bond issuances are repeat transactions. Where parties expect to have repeated transactions, the risk of self-dealing by one party is constrained by the threat that the other party will punish the cheating party in future transactions. The issuer's management has a strong self-interest in the corporation's cost of capital (i.e., avoiding takeovers, maximizing personal wealth, avoiding firm failure). Management therefore will be slow to do anything that unnecessarily increases their cost of capital. But if they abuse their current bondholders, that will come back to haunt them the next time they want to use the bond market to raise capital. If investors care about protection from insider trading, management therefore will provide it by contract.

In addition, negotiations between the issuer and the underwriters that market the debt securities will produce efficient levels of protection. Because the bond market is dominated by a small number of institutional investors, the relationship between underwriters and bondholders is another example of the repeat transaction phenomenon. Underwriters will not sully their reputations with bondholders for the sake of one issuer. Moreover, in a firm commitment underwriting, the underwriters buy the securities from the issuer. If the indenture does not provide adequate levels of protection, the underwriters will be unable to sell the bonds. Again, if debtholders care about insider trading, the contract will prohibit it.

The Post–*Chiarella* Gaps

Chiarella created a variety of significant gaps in the insider trading prohibition's coverage. Consider the Gilda Gekko example from the hypotheticals set forth supra pages 56–57: Gekko's law firm was hired by Ajax to represent it in connection with a planned takeover bid for Acme. Before Ajax publicly disclosed its intentions, Gekko purchased a substantial block of Acme stock.

Under the classic disclose or abstain rule, Gekko has not violated the insider trading prohibition. Whatever duties she owed Ajax, she owed no duty to the shareholders of Acme. Like Vincent Chiarella, she is a stranger to them. Accordingly, the requisite breach of fiduciary duty is not present in her transaction. Rule 14e–3 and the misappropriation theory were created to fill this gap.

The Misappropriation Theory

The misappropriation theory's origins are commonly traced to Chief Justice Burger's *Chiarella* dissent. Burger contended that the way in which the inside trader acquires the nonpublic information on which he trades could itself be a material circumstance that must be disclosed to the market before trading. Accordingly, he argued, "a person who has misappropriated nonpublic information has an absolute duty [to the persons with whom he trades] to disclose that information or to refrain from trading."[90] The majority did not address the

90. *Chiarella v. United States*, 445 U.S. 222, 240 (1980) (Burger, C.J., dissenting).

merits of this theory, instead rejecting it solely on the ground that such a theory had not been presented to the jury and therefore could not sustain a criminal conviction.

The way was thus left open for the SEC to urge and the lower courts to adopt the misappropriation theory as an alternative basis of insider trading liability. In *United States v. Newman*,[91] for example, employees of an investment bank misappropriated confidential information concerning proposed mergers involving clients of the firm. As had been true of Vincent Chiarella, the Newman defendants' employer worked for prospective acquiring companies, while the trading took place in target company securities. As such, the Newman defendants owed no fiduciary duties to the investors with whom they traded. In this instance, moreover, neither the investment bank nor in its clients traded in the target companies' shares contemporaneously with the defendants.

In upholding the *Newman* defendant's convictions, the Second Circuit did not follow Chief Justice Burger's *Chiarella* dissent. It thus did not hold that the defendants owed any duty of disclosure to the investors with whom they traded or had defrauded them. Instead, the court held that by misappropriating confidential information for personal gain, the defendants had defrauded their employer and its clients and that that fraud sufficed to impose insider trading liability on the defendants.

91. 664 F.2d 12 (2d Cir. 1981), cert. denied, 464 U.S. 863 (1983).

Like the traditional disclose or abstain rule, the misappropriation theory requires a breach of fiduciary duty before trading on inside information becomes unlawful.[92] As the *Newman* holding indicates, however, the fiduciary relationship in question is a quite different one. Under the misappropriation theory, the defendant need not owe a fiduciary duty to the investor with whom he trades. Likewise, he need not owe a fiduciary duty to the issuer of the securities that were traded. Instead, the misappropriation theory applies when the inside trader violates a fiduciary duty owed to the source of the information. As eventually refined, the misappropriation theory imposed liability on persons who (1) misappropriated material nonpublic information (2) thereby breaching a fiduciary duty or a duty arising out of a similar relationship of trust and confidence and (3) used that information in securities transaction, regardless of whether they owed any duties to the shareholders of the company in whose stock they traded. If the misappropriation theory had been available against Chiarella, for example, his conviction could have been upheld even though he owed no duties to those with whom he had traded. Instead, the breach of the duty he owed to Pandick Press would have sufficed.

92. See *SEC v. Switzer*, 590 F.Supp. 756, 766 (W.D.Okla. 1984) (not unlawful to trade on the basis of inadvertently overheard information).

The Supreme Court first took up the misappropriation theory in *Carpenter v. United States*,[93] in which a Wall Street Journal reporter and his confederates misappropriated information belonging to the Journal. The Supreme Court upheld the resulting convictions under the mail and wire fraud statutes, holding that confidential business information is property protected by those statutes from being taken by trick, deceit, or chicanery. As to the defendants' securities fraud convictions, however, the court split 4–4. Following the long-standing tradition governing evenly divided Supreme Court decisions, the lower court ruling was affirmed without opinion, but that ruling had no precedential or stare decisis value.

The way was thus left open for lower courts to reject the misappropriation theory, which the Fourth and Eighth Circuits subsequently did in, respectively, *United States v. Bryan*[94] and *United States v. O'Hagan*.[95] These courts held that Rule 10b–5 imposed liability only where there has been deception upon the purchaser or seller of securities, or upon some other person intimately linked with or affected by a securities transaction. Because the misappropriation theory involves no such deception, but rather simply a breach of fiduciary duty owed to the source of the information, the theory could not stand. The Supreme Court took cert. in *United States v. O'Hagan* to resolve the resulting split

93. 484 U.S. 19 (1987).

94. 58 F.3d 933 (4th Cir.1995).

95. 92 F.3d 612 (8th Cir.1996), rev'd, 521 U.S. 642 (1997).

between these circuits and the prior Second Circuit holdings validating the misappropriation theory.

O'Hagan Facts

James O'Hagan was a partner in the Minneapolis law firm of Dorsey & Whitney. In July 1988, Grand Metropolitan PLC (Grand Met), retained Dorsey & Whitney in connection with its planned takeover of Pillsbury Company. Although O'Hagan was not one of the lawyers on the Grand Met project, he learned of their intentions and began buying Pillsbury stock and call options on Pillsbury stock. When Grand Met announced its tender offer in October, the price of Pillsbury stock nearly doubled, allowing O'Hagan to reap a profit of more than $4.3 million.

O'Hagan was charged with violating 1934 Act § 10(b) and Rule 10b–5 by trading on misappropriated nonpublic information. As with Chiarella and the *Newman* defendants, and Gilda Gekko from our hypotheticals, O'Hagan could not be held liable under the disclose or abstain rule as a constructive insider because he worked for the bidder but traded in target company stock. He was neither a classic insider nor a constructive insider of the issuer of the securities in which he traded.[96]

96. O'Hagan was also indicted for violations of Rule 14e–3, which proscribes insider trading in connection with tender offers, and the federal mail fraud and money laundering statutes. The Eighth Circuit overturned O'Hagan's convictions under those provisions. As to Rule 14e–3, the court held that the SEC lacked authority to adopt a prohibition of insider trading that does not require a breach of fiduciary duty. *O'Hagan*, 92 F.3d at 622–27. As to O'Hagan's mail fraud and money laundering convictions,

The Issues

Both § 10(b) and Rule 10b–5 sweep broadly, capturing "any" fraudulent or manipulative conduct "in connection with" the purchase or sale of "any" security. Despite the almost breathtaking expanse of regulatory authority Congress thereby delegated to the Commission, the Supreme Court has warned against expanding the concept of securities fraud beyond that which the words of the statute will reasonably bear. From a textualist perspective, the validity of the misappropriation theory thus depends upon whether (1) the deceit, if any, worked by the misappropriator on the source of the information constitutes deception as the term is used in § 10(b) and Rule 10b–5 and (2) any such deceit is deemed to have occurred "in connection with" the purchase or sale of a security.

Deceit on the source of the information; herein of *Santa Fe*. In *Bryan*, the Fourth Circuit defined fraud—as the term is used in § 10(b) and Rule 10b–5—"as the making of a material misrepresentation or the nondisclosure of material informa-

the Eighth Circuit also reversed them on grounds that the indictment was structured so as to premise the charges under those provisions on the primary securities fraud violations. Id. at 627–28. Accordingly, in view of the court's reversal of the securities fraud convictions, the latter counts could not stand either. The Supreme Court reversed on all points, reinstating O'Hagan's convictions under all of the statutory violations charged in the indictment. *United States v. O'Hagan*, 521 U.S. 642 (1997). The court's Rule 14e–3 holding is discussed infra pages 118–120.

tion in violation of a duty to disclose."[97] So defined, fraud is present in a misappropriation case only in a technical and highly formalistic sense. Although a misappropriator arguably deceives the source of the information, any such deception is quite inconsequential. The source of the information presumably is injured, if at all, not by the deception, but by the conversion of the information by the misappropriator for his own profit. Hence, it is theft—and any concomitant breach of fiduciary duty—by the misappropriator that is truly objectionable. Any deception on the source of the information is purely incidental to the theft. Accordingly, the Fourth Circuit held, the misappropriation theory runs afoul of the Supreme Court's holding in *Santa Fe* that a mere breach of duty cannot give rise to Rule 10b–5 liability: "the misappropriation theory [improperly] transforms § 10(b) from a rule intended to govern and protect relations among market participants who are owed duties under the securities laws into a federal common law governing and protecting any and all trust relationships."

The "in connection with" requirement; herein of *Central Bank*. According to the Eighth Circuit's *O'Hagan* opinion, "the misappropriation theory does not require 'deception,' and, even assuming that it does, it renders nugatory the requirement that the 'deception' be 'in connection with the purchase or sale of any security,'" as required by the text of § 10(b).[98] As such, the

97. 58 F.3d at 946.

98. *O'Hagan*, 92 F.3d at 617.

Eighth Circuit held that the theory ran afoul of the Supreme Court's *Central Bank* decision.

Recall that *Central Bank* held the text of § 10(b) to be dispositive with respect to the scope of conduct regulated by that section. The Eighth Circuit interpreted the statutory prohibition of fraud created by § 10(b) narrowly to exclude conduct constituting a "mere breach of a fiduciary duty," but rather to capture only conduct constituting a material misrepresentation or the nondisclosure of material information in violation of the duty to disclose. Insofar as the misappropriation theory permits the imposition of § 10(b) liability based upon a breach of fiduciary duty without any such deception, the Eighth Circuit held that the theory was inconsistent with the plain statutory text of § 10(b) and, accordingly, invalid as per *Central Bank*.

The Eighth Circuit's principal rationale for rejecting the misappropriation theory, however, was based on the statutory limitation that the fraud be committed "in connection with" a securities transaction. Again relying upon the Supreme Court's *Central Bank* decision, the *O'Hagan* court gave this provision a narrow interpretation. Specifically, the court held that § 10(b) reaches "only a breach of a duty to parties to the securities transaction or, at the most, to other market participants such as investors."[99] Absent such a limitation, the court

99. *O'Hagan*, 92 F.3d at 618. In *Bryan*, the Fourth Circuit similarly opined § 10(b) is primarily concerned with deception of purchasers and sellers of securities, and at most extends to fraud

opined, § 10(b) would be transformed "into an expansive 'general fraud-on-the-source theory' which seemingly would apply infinite number of trust relationships." Such an expansive theory of liability, the court further opined, could not be justified by the text of statute.

In the typical misappropriation case, of course, the source of the information is not the affected purchaser or seller. Often the source is not even a contemporaneous purchaser or seller and frequently has no stake in any affected securities transaction. In *Carpenter*, for example, the Wall Street Journal was neither a purchaser nor seller of the affected securities, nor did it have any financial stake in any of the affected transactions. Similarly, in *Bryan*, the state of West Virginia was not a purchaser or seller, and had no direct stake in Bryan's securities transactions. In neither case did the defendant fail to disclose material information to a market participant to whom he owed a duty of disclosure. One thus must stretch the phrase "in connection with" pretty far in order to bring a misappropriator's alleged fraud within the statute's ambit, even assuming the misappropriator has deceived the source of the information, . As the Fourth Circuit put it: "The misappropriation of information from an individual who is in no way connected to, or even interested in, securities is simply not the kind of conduct with which the securities laws, as presently written, are concerned."

committed against other persons closely linked to, and with a stake in, a securities transaction. 58 F.3d at 946.

The Eighth and Fourth Circuits' interpretation of § 10(b) has much to commend it. The courts carefully considered the Supreme Court's relevant precedents, especially *Santa Fe* and *Central Bank*. Insofar as the misappropriation theory imposes liability solely on the basis of a breach of fiduciary duty to the source of the information, without any requirement that the alleged perpetrator have deceived the persons with whom he traded or other market participants, it arguably ran afoul of those precedents. As the Eighth Circuit opined, the lower court decisions endorsing the misappropriation theory had generally failed to conduct a rigorous analysis of § 10(b)'s text or the pertinent Supreme Court decisions. Indeed, in a telling passage of his partial dissent to a leading Second Circuit opinion endorsing and fleshing out the misappropriation theory, Judge Winter (a former corporate law professor at Yale) stated the misappropriation theory lacked "any obvious relationship" to the statutory text of § 10(b) because "theft rather than fraud or deceit" had become "the gravamen of the prohibition."[100]

Yet, there were problems with applying *Central Bank* to the insider trading prohibition. Although the Fourth Circuit was careful to opine that *Bryan* left intact both the disclose or abstain theory of liability and tipping liability thereunder, arguably this is not the case. As we have seen, the duty at issue in tipping cases is not a duty to disclose, but

100. *United States v. Chestman*, 947 F.2d 551, 578 (2d Cir. 1991), (Winter, J., concurring in part and dissenting in part).

rather, a duty to refrain from self-dealing in confidential information owed by the tipper to the source of the information. As such, tipping is subject to the same line of attack as the Fourth and Eighth Circuits invoked against the misappropriation theory.

Even the basic disclose or abstain theory of liability was called into question by those courts' decisions. Granted, insider trading in violation of the disclose or abstain rule involves an element of deception. By definition, the defendant has failed to disclose nonpublic information before trading. As we have seen, however, the insider trading prohibition generally collapses into a rule to abstain from trading rather than a rule requiring disclosure or abstention. In other words, given that defendant had no right to disclose, it is the failure to abstain from trading, rather than any deception, which is the basis for imposing liability.

Put another way, the claim that insider trading involves deception is circular. As *Chiarella* made clear, and *Dirks* affirmed, not all failures to disclose are fraudulent. Rather, a nondisclosure is actionable only if the trader is subject to a duty to disclose. In turn, a duty to disclose exists only where the trader is subject to a fiduciary duty to refrain from self-dealing in confidential information. Absent such a fiduciary duty, insider trading simply is not fraudulent. Once again, this leaves the disclose or abstain rule subject to the same line of attack as was adopted by the Fourth and Eighth Circuits.

A further problem is that the texts in fact provide little guidance as to the scope of insider trading liability. Recall that under *Central Bank*, where the text does not resolve some aspect of the Rule 10b–5 cause of action, courts must infer how the 1934 Congress would have addressed the issue if Rule 10b–5 had been included as an express provision of the 1934 Act. *Central Bank* somewhat constrained the imaginative process by requiring courts to use the express causes of action in the securities acts as the primary model for interpreting Rule 10b–5. As applied to insider trading, however, this approach is not especially helpful. The short-swing profits cause of action under Section 16(b) of the Exchange Act regulates insider trading only indirectly, does not seek to define insider trading, and does not involve questions of fiduciary duty. Section 20A provides an express private right of action for those who trade contemporaneously with an insider and Section 21A provides a treble money civil fine for insider trading, but both were adopted more than 50 years after Section 10(b) and, moreover, neither provides a substantive definition of insider trading.

Non-textual evidence of congressional intent suggests that extension of *Central Bank* to the insider trading context in fact would be inconsistent with the will of Congress. There is a strong argument that Congress in 1934 did not intend to regulate insider trading in any way other than through the short-swing profit provisions of Section 16(b).[101] Since 1934, however, Congress has twice amended

101. Bainbridge, *State Law*, supra note 68, at 1228–31.

the Exchange Act for the specific purpose of enhancing the penalties associated with insider trading.[102] On both occasions, Congress strongly supported vigorous SEC enforcement of the federal insider trading prohibition.[103] Although ex post facto indications of legislative intent often are viewed skeptically, the recent amendments arguably constitute an authoritative congressional endorsement of the insider trading prohibition generally and the misappropriation theory in particular.

Under the so-called re-enactment doctrine, where Congress has revised a statute without reversing prior on-point judicial holdings, that failure has been taken as evidence of congressional approval of those holdings.[104] In adopting neither the 1984 Insider Trading Sanctions Act nor the 1988 Insider Trading and Securities Fraud Enforcement Act, did Congress see fit to reverse the misappropriation theory. To the contrary, the legislative history of both acts is replete with statements of congressional approval of that theory.[105] Indeed, Section 2 of the 1988 Insider Trading and Securities Enforcement Act provides an express congressional finding that

102. Insider Trading and Securities Fraud Enforcement Act of 1988, Pub. L. No. 100–704, 102 Stat. 4677 (1988); Insider Trading Sanctions Act of 1984, Pub. L. No. 98–376, 98 Stat. 1264 (1984).

103. E.g., H.R. Rep. No. 910, 100th Cong., 2d Sess. 11–16 (1988).

104. See, e.g., *Merrill Lynch, Pierce, Fenner & Smith, Inc. v. Curran*, 456 U.S. 353 (1982).

105. E.g., H.R. Rep. No. 910, supra note 103, at 10, 26; H.R. Rep. No. 355, 98th Cong., 1st Sess. 4–5 (1983).

the SEC's rules "governing trading while in possession of material, nonpublic information are, as required by the Act, necessary and appropriate in the public interest and for the protection of investors."[106] The accompanying House Report further states that "these findings are intended as an expression of congressional support for these regulations."

On the substantive level, the 1988 Act overruled *Moss v. Morgan Stanley, Inc.*,[107] in which the Second Circuit had held that private parties did not have standing to sue under the misappropriation theory. The 1988 Act expressly created a private party cause of action for insider trading cases. Because an implied private party cause of action already existed as to violations of the disclose or abstain rule, however, Congress's action amounts to an express legislative endorsement of the misappropriation theory.

At least insofar as the reenactment doctrine applies to insider trading cases arising under Rule 10b–5, however, *Central Bank* placed it in serious jeopardy. The *Central Bank* majority remarked that arguments based on the re-enactment doctrine "deserve little weight in the interpretive process." The Court also held that because "Congress has not reenacted the language of § 10(b) since 1934" the

106. Pub. L. No. 100–704, 102 Stat. 4677 (1988). As suggested by the congressional use of the plural form, these findings and legislative history apparently were intended to validate SEC Rule 14e–3 as well as the misappropriation theory.

107. 719 F.2d 5 (2d Cir.1983), cert. denied, 465 U.S. 1025 (1984).

Court need not "determine whether the other conditions for applying the reenactment doctrine are present." Hence, even if Congress had intended that the 1984 and 1988 amendments expressly endorse the misappropriation theory, that action arguably would not be binding on the courts.

Extension of this aspect of *Central Bank* to the insider trading context is just as problematic as extension of its main holding thereto. Rejecting the re-enactment doctrine as authority for the misappropriation theory simply because § 10(b) has never been re-enacted ignores highly relevant congressional action elsewhere in the act and thus flouts the apparent congressional intent. If only the intent of the 1934 Congress is relevant, after all, the evidence suggests that § 10(b) was not concerned with insider trading and the prohibition as a whole should be overturned. This would negate the subsequently adopted statutory penalties for insider trading because there no longer would be any underlying violation to which they could be applied, which is an anomalous result, at best. Should penalties Congress adopted with the clear intent that they be applied to misappropriation of information be rendered nugatory by judicial rejection of the underlying cause of action?

In light of these considerations, reconciling the insider trading prohibition with *Central Bank* loomed as one of the major doctrinal problems facing the Supreme Court in *O'Hagan*.

Holding

In *O'Hagan*, a majority of the Supreme Court upheld the misappropriation theory as a valid basis on which to impose insider trading liability. A fiduciary's undisclosed use of information belonging to his principal, without disclosure of such use to the principal, for personal gain constitutes fraud in connection with the purchase or sale of a security, the majority (per Justice Ginsburg) opined, and thus violates Rule 10b–5.[108]

The court acknowledged that misappropriators such as O'Hagan have no disclosure obligation running to the persons with whom they trade. Instead, it grounded liability under the misappropriation theory on deception of the source of the information. As the majority interpreted the theory, it addresses the use of "confidential information for securities trading purposes, in breach of a duty owed to the source of the information." Under this theory, the majority explained, "a fiduciary's undisclosed, self-serving use of a principal's information to purchase or sell securities, in breach of a duty of loyalty and confidentiality, defrauds the principal of

108. *United States v. O'Hagan*, 521 U.S. 642, 117 S.Ct. 2199 (1997). The principal dissent will not go down as one of Justice Thomas' finest moments. It meanders down various inconsequential paths, exploring such momentous questions as whether O'Hagan might have used the information he misappropriated "in a fantasy stock trading game," id. at 2223, while ignoring the very serious policy and statutory interpretation questions posed by the misappropriation theory.

the exclusive use of that information."[109] So defined, the majority held, the misappropriation theory satisfies § 10(b)'s requirement that there be a "deceptive device or contrivance" used "in connection with" a securities transaction.[110]

Status of *Central Bank*: As we have just seen, the tension between *Central Bank* and the insider trading prohibition was a major doctrinal issue facing the court in *O'Hagan*. Surprisingly, however, the majority essentially punted on this issue. The majority essentially ignored both the statutory text, except for some rather glib assertions about the meaning of the phrases "deception" and "in connection with," and the cogent arguments advanced by both the Eighth and Fourth Circuits with respect to the implications of *Central Bank* for the misappropriation theory. To the extent the majority discussed *Central Bank*'s implications for the problem at hand, it focused solely on the Eighth Circuit's argument that *Central Bank* limited Rule 10b–5's regulatory purview to purchasers and sellers. The interpretive methodology expounded in *Central Bank* was essentially ignored. Strikingly, Justice Scalia dissented from the majority's Rule

109. Id.

110. The Supreme Court thus rejected Chief Justice Burger's argument in *Chiarella* that the misappropriation theory created disclosure obligation running to those with whom the misappropriator trades. *O'Hagan*, 117 S.Ct. at 2208 n.6. Instead, it is the failure to disclose one's intentions to the source of the information that constitutes the requisite disclosure violation under the *O'Hagan* version of the misappropriation theory. Id. at 2208.

10b–5 holding, relying on the "unelaborated statutory language." One is therefore left to wonder whether the strict textualist approach taken by *Central Bank* was a one time aberration.

The majority's failure to more carefully evaluate *Central Bank*'s implications for the phrase "in connection with," as used in § 10(b), is especially troubling. By virtue of the majority's holding that deception on the source of the information satisfies the "in connection with" requirement, fraudulent conduct having only tenuous connections to a securities transaction is brought within Rule 10b–5's scope. There has long been a risk that Rule 10b–5 will become a universal solvent, encompassing not only virtually the entire universe of securities fraud, but also much of state corporate law. The minimal contacts *O'Hagan* requires between the fraudulent act and a securities transaction substantially exacerbate that risk. In addition to the risk that much of state corporate law may be preempted by federal developments under Rule 10b–5, the uncertainty created as to Rule 10b–5's parameters fairly raises vagueness and related due process issues, despite the majority's rather glib dismissal of such concerns.

Status of *Santa Fe*: The majority opinion treated *Santa Fe* as a mere disclosure case, asserting: "in *Santa Fe Industries*, all pertinent facts were disclosed by the persons charged with violating § 10(b) and Rule 10b–5; therefore, there was no deception through nondisclosure to which liability under those provisions could attach." The court thus wholly ignored the important federalism concerns upon which *Santa Fe* rested and which are implicated by the misappropriation theory (indeed, by the insider trading prohibition as a whole).

Open questions

In many respects, *O'Hagan* posed more new questions than it answered old ones. Here are some of the more interesting and important issues it left open:

Liability for brazen misappropriators? The *O'Hagan* majority made clear that disclosure to the source of the information is all that is required under Rule 10b–5. If a brazen misappropriator discloses his trading plans to the source, and then trades on that information, Rule 10b–5 is not violated, even if the source of the information refused permission to trade and objected vigorously.[111] If this rule seems odd, so did the majority's justification for it.

According to the majority, "investors likely would hesitate to venture their capital in a market where trading based on misappropriated nonpublic information is unchecked by law." The majority went on to opine that the investor on the other side of the transaction suffers from "a disadvantage that cannot be overcome with research or skill." As such,

111. *O'Hagan*, 117 S. Ct. at 2209 ("full disclosure forecloses liability under the misappropriation theory ... if the fiduciary discloses to the source that he plans to trade on nonpublic information, there is no 'deceptive device' and thus no § 10(b) violation").

the majority claimed that the misappropriation theory advances "an animating purpose of the Exchange Act: to insure [sic] honest securities markets and thereby promote investor confidence."

The difficulties with this argument should be readily apparent. Investors who trade with a brazen misappropriator presumably will not feel any greater confidence in the integrity of the securities market if they later find out that the misappropriator had disclosed his intentions to the source of the information. Worse yet, both the phraseology and the substance of the majority's argument plausibly could be interpreted as resurrecting the long-discredited equal access test. If the goal of insider trading law in fact is to insulate investors from information asymmetries that cannot be overcome by research or skill, the equal access test is far better suited to doing so than the current test.

Merely requiring the prospective misappropriator to disclose his intentions before trading also provides only weak protection of the source of the information's property rights therein. To be sure, because of the disclosure requirement concerns about detecting improper trading are alleviated. As the majority pointed out, moreover, the source may have state law claims against the misappropriator. In particular, the agency law prohibition on the use of confidential information for personal gain will often provide a remedy to the source. In some jurisdictions, however, it is far from clear whether inside trading by a fiduciary violates state law. Even where state law proscribes such trading, the Supreme Court's approach means that in brazen misappropriator cases we lose the comparative advantage the SEC has in litigating insider trading cases and, moreover, also lose the comparative advantage provided by the well-developed and relatively liberal remedy under Rule 10b–5.

Liability for authorized trading? Suppose a takeover bidder authorized an arbitrageur to trade in target company's stock on the basis of material nonpublic information about the perspective bidder's intentions. Warehousing of this sort is proscribed by Rule 14e–3, but only insofar as the information relates to a prospective tender offer. Whether such trading in a non-tender offer context violated Rule 10b–5 was unclear before *O'Hagan*.

The *O'Hagan* majority at least implicitly validated authorized trading. It approvingly quoted, for example, the statement of the government's counsel that "to satisfy the common law rule the trustee may not use the property that [has] been entrusted [to] him, there would have to be consent."

On the facts of *O'Hagan*, as the majority indicated, insiders would need approval from both Dorsey & Whitney and Grand Met in order to escape Rule 10b–5 liability. Is it plausible that Grand Met would have given such approval? Maybe. Warehousing of takeover stocks and tipping acquisition plans to friendly parties were once common—hence the need for Rule 14e–3—and probably still occurs.

Notice the interesting question presented by the requirement that O'Hagan disclose his intentions to

Dorsey & Whitney. Given that O'Hagan was a partner in Dorsey & Whitney, query whether his knowledge of his intentions would be imputed to the firm. As a practical matter, of course, O'Hagan should have informed the lawyer with the principal responsibility for the Grand Met transaction and/or the firm's managing partner.

The authorized trading dictum has significant, but as yet little-noticed, implications. Query, for example, whether it applies to all insider trading cases or just to misappropriation cases. Suppose that in a classic disclose or abstain case, such as *Texas Gulf Sulphur*, the issuer's board of directors adopted a policy of allowing insider trading by managers. If they did so, the corporation has consented to any such inside trading, which under Justice Ginsburg's analysis appears to vitiate any deception. The corporate policy itself presumably would have to be disclosed, just as broad disclosure respecting executive compensation is already required, but the implication is that authorized trading should not result in 10b–5 liability under either misappropriation or disclose or abstain.

On the other hand, the two theories can be distinguished in ways that undermine application of the authorized trading dictum to disclose or abstain cases. In a misappropriation case, such as *Carpenter*, liability is premised on fraud on the source of the information. In *Carpenter*, acting through appropriate decision making processes, the Journal could authorize inside trading by its agents. By contrast, however, *Chiarella* focused the classic disclose or abstain rule on fraud perpetrated on the specific investors with whom the insiders trade. Authorization of inside trading by the issuer's board of directors, or even a majority of the shareholders, does not constitute consent by the specific investors with whom the insider trades. Nothing in *O'Hagan* explicitly suggests an intent to undermine the *Chiarella* interpretation of the traditional disclose or abstain rule. To the contrary, Justice Ginsburg expressly states that the two theories are "complementary." Because the disclose or abstain rule thus remains conceptually distinct from the misappropriation theory, the authorized trading dictum can be plausibly limited to the latter context.

The fiduciary relationship requirement. Does a duty to disclose to the source of the information arise before trading in all fiduciary relationships? Consider ABA Model Rule of Professional Conduct 1.8(b), which states: "A lawyer shall not use information relating to representation of a client to the disadvantage of the client unless the client consents after consultation...." Does a lawyer's use of confidential client information for insider trading purposes always operate to the client's disadvantage? If not, and assuming the Model Rule accurately states the lawyer's fiduciary obligation, O'Hagan did not violate § 10(b).

The *O'Hagan* majority, however, failed to inquire into the nature of O'Hagan's duties, if any, to Grand Met. Instead, the majority assumed that lawyers are fiduciaries, all fiduciaries are subject to a duty to refrain from self-dealing in confidential information, and, accordingly, that the misappropriation theory applies to lawyers and all other fiduciaries. The majority's approach, of course, begs the question—how do we know O'Hagan is a fiduciary? We touched on this problem in our discussion of who is an insider, supra pages 77–82. As we saw, there remains no definitive answer to this problem.

Criminal or civil? In rejecting the Eighth Circuit's argument that Rule 10b–5 is primarily concerned with deception of market participants, the majority noted that the discussion in *Central Bank* upon which the Eighth Circuit relied dealt only with private civil litigation under § 10(b). The court then went on to discuss its holding in *Blue Chip Stamps*[112] that only actual purchasers or sellers of securities have standing to bring private causes of action under Rule 10b–5. The court concluded: "Criminal prosecutions do not present the dangers the Court addressed in *Blue Chip Stamps*, so that decision is 'inapplicable' to indictments for violations of § 10(b) and Rule 10b–5."

This passage opens the door for misappropriators to argue that *O'Hagan* should be limited to criminal prosecutions, because the majority acknowledged the limitations imposed by *Central Bank* and *Blue Chip Stamps* on private party litigation. Such a limitation on private party in litigation, however, seems unlikely. Although the majority declined to address the significance of the 1988 statute and its legislative history for the validity of the misappro-

112. *Blue Chip Stamps v. Manor Drug Stores*, 421 U.S. 723 (1975).

priation theory, interpreting *O'Hagan* as validating the misappropriation theory only as to criminal actions would render the private party cause of action created by Exchange Act § 20A nugatory.

Rule 14e–3

The SEC adopted Rule 14e–3 in response to the wave of insider trading activity associated with the increase in merger and acquisition activity during the 1980s. The rule prohibits insiders of the bidder and target from divulging confidential information about a tender offer to persons that are likely to violate the rule by trading on the basis of that information. This provision (Rule 14e–3(d)(1)) does not prohibit the bidder from buying target shares or from telling its legal and financial advisers about its plans. What the rule prohibits is tipping of information to persons who are likely to buy target shares for their own account. In particular, the rule was intended to strike at the practice known as warehousing. Anecdotal evidence suggests that before Rule 14e–3 was on the books bidders frequently tipped their intentions to friendly parties. Warehousing increased the odds a hostile takeover bid would succeed by increasing the number of shares likely to support the bidder's proposal.

Rule 14e–3 also, with certain narrow and well-defined exceptions, prohibits any person that possesses material information relating to a tender offer by another person from trading in target company securities if the bidder has commenced or has taken substantial steps towards commencement of the bid. Substantial steps include such things as voting on a resolution by the offering person's board of directors relating to the tender offer; the formulation of a plan or proposal to make a tender offer by the offering person; or activities which substantially facilitate the tender offer such as: arranging financing for a tender offer; preparing or directing or authorizing the preparation of tender offer materials. The trader must know or have reason to know that the information is nonpublic. The trader also must know or have reason to know the information was acquired from the bidder or the target company or agents of either.

Unlike both the disclose or abstain rule and the misappropriation theory under Rule 10b–5, Rule 14e–3 liability is not premised on breach of a fiduciary duty. There is no need for a showing that the trading party or tipper was subject to any duty of confidentiality, and no need to show that a tipper personally benefited from the tip. In light of the well-established fiduciary duty requirement under Rule 10b–5, however, the rule arguably ran afoul of *Schreiber v. Burlington Northern, Inc.*,[113] in which the Supreme Court held that § 14(e) was modeled on § 10(b) and, like that section, requires a showing of misrepresentation or nondisclosure. If the two sections are to be interpreted in pari materia, as *Shreiber* indicated, and § 10(b) requires a showing of a breach of a duty in order for liability to arise, the SEC appeared to have exceeded its statutory authority by adopting a rule that makes illegal a

113. 472 U.S. 1 (1985).

variety of trading practices that do not involve any breach of duty. In *United States v. O'Hagan*,[114] however, the Supreme Court upheld Rule 14e–3 as a valid exercise of the SEC's rulemaking authority despite the absence of a fiduciary duty element.

Notice that Rule 14e–3 nonetheless is quite limited in scope. One prong of the rule (the prohibition on trading while in possession of material nonpublic information) does not apply until the offeror has taken substantial steps towards making the offer. More important, both prongs of the rule are limited to information relating to a tender offer. As a result, most types of inside information remain subject to the duty-based analysis of *Chiarella* and its progeny.

Although most lawsuits under 14e–3 have been brought by the SEC, most courts to address the issue have concluded that a private right of action exists under the rule and is available to investors trading in the target's securities at the same time as the persons who violated the rule.

Remedies and Penalties

Woe unto those who violate the insider trading prohibition, for the penalties are many, cumulative, and severe. The Justice Department may pursue criminal charges. The SEC may pursue a variety of civil penalties. Private party litigants may bring damage actions under both federal and state law.

114.   521 U.S. 642, 117 S.Ct. 2199, 2214–19 (1997).

The SEC has no authority to prosecute criminal actions against inside traders, but it is authorized by Exchange Act § 21(d)(1) to ask the Justice Department to initiate a criminal prosecution. In addition, the Justice Department may bring such a prosecution on its own initiative. Under § 32(a), a willful violation of Rule 10b–5 or 14e–3 is a felony that can be punished by a $1 million fine ($2.5 in the case of corporations) and up to 10 years in jail. Since the mid–1980s insider trading scandals, criminal prosecutions have become fairly common in this area.

The SEC long has had the authority to pursue various civil penalties in insider trading cases. Under Exchange Act § 21(d), the SEC may seek a permanent or temporary injunction whenever "it shall appear to the Commission that any person is engaged or is about to engage in any acts or practices constituting a violation" of the Act or any rules promulgated thereunder. Courts have made it quite easy for the SEC to obtain injunctions under § 21(d). The SEC must make a "proper showing," but that merely requires the SEC to demonstrate a violation of the securities laws occurred and there is a reasonable likelihood of future violations.[115] The SEC is not required to meet traditional requirements for equitable relief, such as irreparable

115. See *SEC v. Commonwealth Chem. Sec., Inc.*, 574 F.2d 90, 99–100 (2d Cir.1978). But cf. *SEC v. Lund*, 570 F.Supp. 1397, 1404 (C.D.Cal.1983) (court denied an injunction on the grounds that the defendant's action was "an isolated occurrence" and that his "profession [was] not likely to lead him into future violations").

harm.[116] The SEC is not required to identify particular individuals who were wronged by the conduct, moreover, but only that the violation occurred.

"Once the equity jurisdiction of the district court has been properly invoked by the showing of a securities law violation, the court possesses the necessary power to fashion an appropriate remedy."[117] Thus, in addition to or in place of injunctive relief, the SEC may seek disgorgement of profits, correction of misleading statements, disclosure of material information, or other special remedies. Of these, disgorgement of profits to the government is the most commonly used enforcement tool.

The SEC may also punish insider trading by regulated market professionals through administrative proceedings. Under § 15(b)(4) of the 1934 Act, the SEC may censure, limit the activities of, suspend, or revoke the registration of a broker or dealer who willfully violates the insider trading prohibition. Similar sanctions may be imposed on those associated with the broker or dealer in such activities. The SEC may issue a report of its investigation of the incident even if it decides not to pursue judicial or administrative proceedings, which may lead to private litigation.

During the 1980s, Congress significantly expanded the civil sanctions available to the SEC for use

116. See *SEC v. Management Dynamics, Inc.*, 515 F.2d 801 (2d Cir.1975); *SEC v. Manor Nursing Centers, Inc.*, 458 F.2d 1082 (2d Cir.1972).

117. *SEC v. Manor Nursing Centers*, 458 F.2d 1082, 1103 (2d Cir.1972).

against inside traders. The Insider Trading Sanctions Act of 1984 created a civil monetary penalty of up to three times the profit gained or loss avoided by a person who violates rules 10b–5 or 14e–3 "by purchasing or selling a security while in the possession of material non-public information." An action to impose such a penalty may be brought in addition to or in lieu of any other actions that the SEC or Justice Department is entitled to bring. Because the SEC thus may seek both disgorgement and treble damages, an inside trader faces potential civil liability of up to four times the profit gained.

In the Insider Trading and Securities Fraud Act of 1988 (ITSFEA), Congress made a number of further changes designed to augment the enforcement resources and penalties available to the SEC. Among other things, it authorized the SEC to pay a bounty to informers of up to 10 percent of any penalty collected by the SEC. The treble money fine was extended to controlling persons, so as to provide brokerage houses, for example, with greater incentives to monitor the activities of their employees.

Although it has long been clear that persons who traded contemporaneously with an inside trader have a private cause of action under Rule 10b–5 (and perhaps Rule 14e–3), and may also have state law claims, private party litigation against inside traders has been rare and usually parasitic on SEC enforcement actions. Private party actions were further discouraged by the Second Circuit's decision in

Moss v. Morgan Stanley, Inc.,[118] which held that contemporaneous traders could not bring private causes of actions under the misappropriation theory. ITSFEA attempted to encourage private actions by overruling *Moss*. Under Exchange Act § 20A, contemporaneous traders can sue to recover up to the amount of profit gained or loss avoided. Tippers and tippees are jointly and severally liable. The amount recoverable is reduced by any amounts disgorged to the Commission. As yet, however, it does not appear that plaintiffs have made very frequent use of § 20A.

118.   719 F.2d 5 (2d Cir.1983).

CHAPTER 4

WHY DO WE CARE? THE ECONOMICS OF INSIDER TRADING

The federal insider trading prohibition has not been cheap. The SEC and other law enforcement agencies have expended vast resources to detect and prosecute inside traders. The lives of those caught have been devastated. Courts have devoted considerable judicial resources to working out and applying the prohibition in all its intricate detail. Has it been worth it?

The policy case against insider trading traditionally sounded in the language of equity. In *Cady, Roberts*, for example, the SEC justified the prohibition as necessary to "the inherent unfairness" of insider trading. But why is insider trading unfair? In *Texas Gulf Sulphur*, the Second Circuit opined that all investors were entitled to "relatively equal access to material information." But whence comes this entitlement? The difficulty, of course, is that fairness and equality are high-sounding but essentially content-less words. We need some standard of reference by which to measure the fairness or lack thereof of insider trading.

In the search for an appropriate reference standard, the seminal event was the 1966 publication of

125

Henry Manne's book INSIDER TRADING AND THE STOCK MARKET. It is only a slight exaggeration to suggest that Manne stunned the corporate law world by daring to propose the deregulation of insider trading. The response by most law professors, lawyers, and regulators was immediate and vitriolic rejection.

In one sense, Manne's project failed. Insider trading is still prohibited. Indeed, as we have seen, the sanctions for violating the prohibition have become more draconian—not less—since Manne's book was first published. In another sense, however, Manne's daring was at least partially vindicated. He changed the terms of the debate. Today, the insider trading debate takes place almost exclusively in the language of economics. Even those who still insist on treating insider trading as an issue of fairness necessarily spend much of their time responding to those who see it in economic terms.

In essence, the argument of Manne and those subsequent scholars who also embraced the idea of deregulating insider trading is that insider trading promotes market efficiency and creates efficient incentives for innovative corporate managers. Those scholars who favor regulating insider trading typically respond either by relying on fairness arguments or by asserting that insider trading has substantial economic costs. In this chapter, we first take up the economic argument for deregulation. We then evaluate the noneconomic arguments for regulating insider trading. Finally, we evaluate the economic arguments for the pro-regulation position.

In each case, we will ask two questions: Does the argument make sense? Can it explain the prohibition as it exists?

A pedagogical caveat—indeed, a warning—is in order: No effort will be made herein to hide the ball. Although this chapter canvases the major arguments for and against all three positions, my own view is that the insider trading prohibition can be justified, but only by an economic argument that treats insider trading as theft of confidential information in which someone other than the inside trader has a property right superior to that of the inside trader. This chapter concludes with an assessment of the implications of that policy position for the proper scope and content of the insider trading prohibition.

The Case for Deregulation

Manne identified two principal ways in which insider trading benefits society and/or the firm in whose stock the insider traded. First, he argued that insider trading causes the market price of the affected security to move toward the price that the security would command if the inside information were publicly available. If so, both society and the firm benefit through increased price accuracy. Second, he posited insider trading as an efficient way of compensating managers for having produced information. If so, the firm benefits directly (and society indirectly) because managers have a greater incentive to produce additional information of value to the firm.

In the years since Manne first wrote, a third argument for deregulating insider trading has been advanced by other scholars. Drawing on the public choice branch of law and economics, this line of argument contends that the prohibition benefits special interest groups. The SEC had institutional incentives to sell a prohibition of insider trading, so the story goes, while certain stock market players had an incentive to purchase such a prohibition.

Insider Trading and Efficient Pricing of Securities

Basic economic theory tells us that the value of a share of stock is simply the present discounted value of the stream of dividends that will be paid on the stock in the future. Because the future is uncertain, however, the amount of future dividends, if any, cannot be known. In an efficient capital market, a security's current price thus is simply the consensus guess of investors as to the issuing corporation's future prospects. The "correct" price of a security is that which would be set by the market if all information relating to the security had been publicly disclosed. Because the market cannot value nonpublic information and because corporations (or outsiders) frequently possess material information that has not been made public, however, market prices often deviate from the "correct" price. Indeed, if it were not for this sort of mispricing, insider trading would not be profitable.

No one seriously disputes that both firms and society benefit from accurate pricing of securities.

Accurate pricing benefits society by improving the economy's allocation of capital investment and by decreasing the volatility of security prices. This dampening of price fluctuations decreases the likelihood of individual windfall gains and increases the attractiveness of investing in securities for risk-averse investors. The individual corporation also benefits from accurate pricing of its securities through reduced investor uncertainty and improved monitoring of management's effectiveness.

Although U.S. securities laws purportedly encourage accurate pricing by requiring disclosure of corporate information, they do not require the disclosure of all material information. Where disclosure would interfere with legitimate business transactions, disclosure by the corporation is usually not required unless the firm is dealing in its own securities at the time.

When a firm withholds material information, its securities are no longer accurately priced by the market. In *Texas Gulf Sulphur*, when the ore deposit was discovered, TGS common stock sold for approximately eighteen dollars per share. By the time the discovery was disclosed, four months later, the price had risen to over thirty-one dollars per share. One month after disclosure, the stock was selling for approximately fifty-eight dollars per share. The difficulty, of course, is that TGS had gone to considerable expense to identify potential areas for mineral exploration and to conduct the initial search. Suppose TGS was required to disclose the ore strike as soon as the initial assay results came back. What would have happened? Landowners would have demanded a higher price for the mineral rights. Worse yet, competitors could have come into the area and bid against TGS for the mineral rights. In economic terms, these competitors would "free ride" on TGS's efforts. TGS will not earn a profit on the ore deposit until it has extracted enough ore to pay for its exploration costs. Because competitors will not have to incur any of the search costs TGS had incurred to find the ore deposit, they will have a higher profit margin on any ore extracted. In turn, that will allow them to outbid TGS for the mineral rights.[119] A securities law rule requiring immediate disclosure of the ore deposit (or any similar proprietary information) would discourage innovation and discovery by permitting this sort of free riding behavior— rational firms would not try to develop new mines if they knew competitors will be able to free ride on their efforts. In order to encourage innovation, the securities laws therefore generally permit corporations to delay disclosure of this sort of information for some period of time. As we have seen, however, the trade-off mandated by this policy is one of less accurate securities prices.

Manne essentially argued that insider trading is an effective compromise between the need for pre-

119. Suppose TGS spent $2 per acre on exploration costs and is willing to pay $10 per acre to buy the mineral rights from the landowners. TGS must make at least $12 per acre on extracted ore before it makes a profit. Because competitors do not incur any exploration costs, they could pay $11 per acre for the mineral rights and still make a profit.

serving incentives to produce information and the need for maintaining accurate securities prices. Manne offered the following example of this alleged effect: A firm's stock currently sells at fifty dollars per share. The firm has discovered new information that, if publicly disclosed, would cause the stock to sell at sixty dollars. If insiders trade on this information, the price of the stock will gradually rise toward the correct price. Absent insider trading or leaks, the stock's price will remain at fifty dollars until the information is publicly disclosed and then rapidly rise to the correct price of sixty dollars. Thus, insider trading acts as a replacement for public disclosure of the information, preserving market gains of correct pricing while permitting the corporation to retain the benefits of nondisclosure.[120]

Despite the anecdotal support for Manne's position provided by *Texas Gulf Sulphur* and similar cases,[121] empirical evidence on point remains scanty. Early market studies indicated insider trading had an insignificant effect on price in most cases.[122] Subsequent studies suggested the market

120. HENRY MANNE, INSIDER TRADING AND THE STOCK MARKET 77–91 (1966).

121. Recall that the TGS insiders began active trading in its stock almost immediately after discovery of the ore deposit. During the four months between discovery and disclosure, the price of TGS common stock gradually rose by over twelve dollars. Arguably, this price increase was due to inside trading. In turn, the insiders' profits were the price society paid for obtaining the beneficial effects of enhanced market efficiency.

122. See Roy A. Schotland, *Unsafe at Any Price*, 53 Va. L. Rev. 1425, 1443 (1967) (citing studies).

reacts fairly quickly when insiders buy securities, but the initial price effect is small when insiders sell.[123] These studies are problematic, however, because they relied principally (or solely) on the transactions reports corporate officers, directors, and 10% shareholders are required to file under Section 16(a).[124] Because insiders are unlikely to report transactions that violate Rule 10b–5, and because much illegal insider trading activity is known to involve persons not subject to the § 16(a) reporting requirement, conclusions drawn from such studies may not tell us very much about the price and volume effects of illegal insider trading. Accordingly, it is significant that a more recent and widely-cited study of insider trading cases brought by the SEC during the 1980s found that the defendants' insider trading led to quick price changes.[125] That result supports Manne's empirical claim, subject to the caveat that reliance on data obtained from SEC prosecutions arguably may not be conclusive as to the price effects of undetected insider trading due to selection bias, although the study in question admittedly made strenuous efforts to avoid any such bias.

Evaluating the efficient pricing thesis requires a brief digression into efficient capital market theory.

123. Dan Givoly & Dan Palmon, *Insider Trading and the Exploitation of Inside Information: Some Empirical Evidence*, 58 J. Bus. 69 (1985).

124. See Chapter 5, infra.

125. Lisa Meulbrock, *An Empirical Analysis of Illegal Insider Trading*, 47 J. Fin. 1661 (1992).

Along with the portfolio theory and the theory of the firm, the efficient capital markets hypothesis has been one of the three economic theories most influential on corporate and securities law. In brief, the hypothesis asserts that in an efficient market current prices always and fully reflect all relevant information about the commodities being traded. In other words, in an efficient market, commodities are never overpriced or under-priced: the current price is an accurate reflection of the market's consensus as to the commodity's value. Of course, there is no real world condition like this, but the securities markets are widely believed to be close to this ideal.

The so-called semi-strong form of the hypothesis posits that current prices incorporate all publicly available information.[126] The semi-strong form predicts that prices will change only if the information is new. If the information had been previously leaked, or anticipated, the price will not change. If correct, investors cannot expect to profit from studying available information because the market

126. The weak form holds that all information concerning historical prices is fully reflected in the current price. Put another way, the weak form predicts that price changes in securities are serially independent or random. Randomness does not mean that we cannot predict whether the stock will go up or down—obviously stock prices generally go up on good news and down on bad news. What randomness means is that investors can not profit by using past prices to predict future prices. Accordingly, it predicts (and the evidence appears to confirm) that charting—the attempt to predict future prices by looking at the past history of stock prices—cannot be a profitable trading strategy over time.

will have already incorporated the information accurately into the price.

The strong form of the hypothesis holds that prices incorporate all information, whether publicly available or not. The strong form makes no intuitive sense: how can the market, which after all is not some omnipotent supernatural being but simply the aggregate of all investors, value information it does not know. If the strong form were true, moreover, insider trading could not be a profitable trading strategy.

Empirical tests of the hypothesis have generally tended to confirm the semi-strong form, while disproving the strong form. To be sure, the validity of the efficient capital markets hypothesis is still hotly debated in academic circles. It is probably fair to say, however, that most scholars regard it as the best available description of how markets behave.

In an efficient market, how does insider trading affect stock prices? Although Manne's assertion that insider trading moves stock prices in the "correct" direction—i.e., the direction the stock price would move if the information were announced—seems intuitively plausible, the anonymity of impersonal market transactions makes it far from obvious that insider trading will have any effect on prices. Accordingly, we need to look more closely at the way in which insider trading might work its magic on stock prices.

If you studied price theory in economics, your initial intuition may be that insider trading affects stock prices by changing the demand for the issuing corporation's stock. Economics tells us that the price of a commodity is set by supply and demand forces. The equilibrium or market clearing price is that at which consumers are willing to buy all of the commodity offered by suppliers. If the supply remains constant, but demand goes up, the equilibrium price rises and vice-versa.

Suppose an insider buys stock on good news. The supply of stock remains constant (assuming the company is not in the midst of a stock offering or repurchase), but demand has increased, so a higher equilibrium price should result. All of which seems perfectly plausible, but for the inconvenient fact that a given security represents only a particular combination of expected return and systematic risk, for which there is a vast number of substitutes. The correct measure for the supply of securities thus is not simply the total of the firm's outstanding securities, but the vastly larger number of securities with a similar combination of risk and return. Accordingly, the supply/demand effect of a relatively small number of insider trades should not have a significant price effect. Over the portion of the curve observed by individual traders, the demand curve should be flat rather than downward sloping.

Instead, if insider trading is to affect the price of securities it is through the derivatively informed trading mechanism of market efficiency. Derivatively informed trading affects market prices through a two-step mechanism. First, those individuals possessing material nonpublic information begin trading. Their trading has only a small effect on price. Some uninformed traders become aware of the insider trading through leakage or tipping of information or through observation of insider trades. Other traders gain insight by following the price fluctuations of the securities. Finally, the market reacts to the insiders' trades and gradually moves toward the correct price. The problem is that while derivatively informed trading can affect price, it functions slowly and sporadically. Given the inefficiency of derivatively informed trading, the market efficiency justification for insider trading loses much of its force.

Insider Trading as an Efficient Compensation Scheme

Manne's other principal argument against the ban on insider trading rested on the claim that allowing insider trading was an effective means of compensating entrepreneurs in large corporations. Manne distinguished corporate entrepreneurs from mere corporate managers. The latter simply operate the firm according to predetermined guidelines. By contrast, an entrepreneur's contribution to the firm consists of producing new valuable information. The entrepreneur's compensation must have a reasonable relation to the value of his contribution to give him incentives to produce more information. Because it is rarely possible to ascertain information's value to the firm in advance, predetermined compensation, such as salary, is inappropriate for entrepreneurs. Instead, claimed Manne, insider trading is an effective way to compensate entrepreneurs for innovations. The increase in the price of the security following public disclosure provides an imperfect but comparatively accurate measure of the value of the innovation to the firm. The entrepreneur can recover the value of his discovery by purchasing the firm's securities prior to disclosure and selling them after the price rises.[127]

Professors Carlton and Fischel subsequently suggested a further refinement of Manne's compensation argument. They likewise believed ex ante contracts fail to appropriately compensate agents for innovations. The firm could renegotiate these contracts ex post to reward innovations, but renegotiation is costly and subject to strategic behavior. One of the advantages of insider trading, they argued, is that an agent revises his compensation package without renegotiating his contract. By trading on the new information, the agent self-tailors his com-

---

127. Manne, supra note 120, at 131–41. In evaluating compensation-based justifications for deregulating inside trading, it is highly relevant to consider whether the corporation or the manager owns the property right to the information in question. Some of those who favor deregulating insider trading deny that firms have a property interest in information produced by their agents that includes the right to prevent the agent from trading on the basis of that information. In contrast, those who favor regulation contend that when an agent produces information the property right to that information belongs to the firm. As described infra pages 164–69, that latter appears to be the better view. The implication of that conclusion for the compensation debate is that agents should not be allowed to set their own compensation by inside trading. Instead, if insider trading is to be used as a form of compensation, it should be so used only with the consent of the firm.

pensation to account for the information he produces, increasing his incentive to develop valuable innovations.[128]

Manne argued salary and bonuses provide inadequate incentives for entrepreneurial inventiveness because they fail to accurately measure the value to the firm of innovations.[129] Query, however, whether insider trading is any more accurate. Even assuming the change in stock price accurately measures the value of the innovation, the insider's compensation is limited by the number of shares he can purchase. This, in turn, is limited by his wealth. As such, the insider's trading returns are based, not on the value of his contribution, but on his wealth.

Another objection to the compensation argument is the difficulty of restricting trading to those who produced the information. Where information is concerned, production costs normally exceed distribution costs. As such, many firm agents may trade on the information without having contributed to its production.

A related criticism is the difficulty of limiting trading to instances in which the insider actually produced valuable information. In particular, why

128. Dennis W. Carlton and Daniel R. Fischel, *The Regulation of Insider Trading*, 35 Stan. L. Rev. 857 (1983). But see Frank H. Easterbrook, *Insider Trading, Secret Agents, Evidentiary Privileges, and the Production of Information*, 1981 Sup. Ct. Rev. 309 (1981); Saul Levmore, *Securities and Secrets: Insider Trading and the Law of Contracts*, 68 Va. L. Rev. 117 (1982); Saul Levmore, *In Defense of the Regulation of Insider Trading*, 11 Harv. J. L. & Pub. Pol. 101 (1988).

129. Manne, supra note 120, at 134–38.

should insiders be permitted to trade on bad news?
Allowing managers to profit from inside trading
reduces the penalties associated with a project's
failure because trading managers can profit whether the project succeeds or fails. If the project fails,
the manager can sell his shares before that information becomes public and thus avoid an otherwise
certain loss. The manager can go beyond mere loss
avoidance into actual profitmaking by short selling
the firm's stock.

A final objection to the compensation thesis follows from the contingent nature of insider trading.
Because the agent's trading returns cannot be mea-
sured in advance, neither can the true cost of his
reward. As a result, selection of the most cost-
effective compensation package is made more difficult. Moreover, the agent himself may prefer a less
uncertain compensation package. If an agent is risk
averse, he will prefer the certainty of $100,000
salary to a salary of $50,000 and a ten percent
chance of a bonus of $500,000 from insider trading.
Thus, the shareholders and the agent would gain by
exchanging a guaranteed bonus for the agent's
promise not to trade on inside information.

Public Choice

Some critics of the insider trading prohibition
contend that the prohibition can be explained by a
public choice-based model of regulation in which
rules are sold by regulators and bought by the

beneficiaries of the regulation.[130] On the supply side, the federal insider trading prohibition may be viewed as the culmination of two distinct trends in the securities laws. First, as do all government agencies, the SEC desired to enlarge its jurisdiction and enhance its prestige. Administrators can maximize their salaries, power, and reputation by maximizing the size of their agency's budget. A vigorous enforcement program directed at a highly visible and unpopular law violation is surely an effective means of attracting political support for larger budgets. Given the substantial media attention directed towards insider trading prosecutions, and the public taste for prohibiting insider trading, it provided a very attractive subject for such a program.

Second, during the prohibition's formative years, there was a major effort to federalize corporation law. In order to maintain its budgetary priority over competing agencies, the SEC wanted to play a major role in federalizing matters previously within the state domain. Insider trading was an ideal target for federalization. Rapid expansion of the federal insider trading prohibition purportedly demon-

130. This section focuses on slightly different, but wholly compatible, stories about insider trading told by Professor Michael Dooley and Professors David Haddock and Jonathan Macey. Dooley's version explains why the SEC wanted to sell insider trading regulation, while Haddock and Macey's explains to whom it has been sold. See MICHAEL P. DOOLEY, FUNDAMENTALS OF CORPORATION LAW 816–57 (1995); David D. Haddock and Jonathan R. Macey, *Regulation on Demand: A Private Interest Model, with an Application to Insider Trading*, 30 J.L. & Econ. 311 (1987); see also JONATHAN R. MACEY, INSIDER TRADING: ECONOMICS, POLITICS, AND POLICY (1991).

strated the superiority of federal securities law over state corporate law. Because the states had shown little interest in insider trading for years, federal regulation demonstrated the modernity, flexibility, and innovativeness of the securities laws. The SEC's prominent role in attacking insider trading thus placed it in the vanguard of the movement to federalize corporate law and ensured that the SEC would have a leading role in any system of federal corporations law.

The validity of this hypothesis is suggested by its ability to explain the SEC's devotion of significant enforcement resources to insider trading during the 1980s. During that decade, the SEC embarked upon a limited program of deregulating the securities markets. Among other things, the SEC adopted a safe harbor for projections and other soft data, the shelf registration rule, the integrated disclosure system, and expanded the exemptions from registration under the Securities Act. At about the same time, however, the SEC adopted a vigorous enforcement campaign against insider trading. Not only did the number of cases increase substantially, but the SEC adopted a "big bang" approach under which it focused on high visibility cases that would produce substantial publicity. In part this may have been due to an increase in the frequency of insider trading, but the public choice story nicely explains the SEC's interest in insider trading as motivated by a desire to preserve its budget during an era of deregulation and spending restraint.

The public choice story also explains the SEC's continuing attachment to the equal access approach to insider trading. The equal access policy generates an expansive prohibition, which federalizes a broad range of conduct otherwise left to state corporate law, while also warranting a highly active enforcement program. As such, the SEC's use of Rule 14e–3 and the misappropriation theory to evade *Chiarella* and *Dirks* makes perfect sense. By these devices, the SEC restored much of the prohibition's pre-*Chiarella* breadth and thereby ensured that its budget-justifying enforcement program would continue unimpeded.

Turning to the demand side, the insider trading prohibition appears to be supported and driven in large part by market professionals, a cohesive and politically powerful interest group, which the current legal regime effectively insulates from insider trading liability. Only insiders and quasi-insiders such as lawyers and investment bankers have greater access to material nonpublic information than do market professionals. By basing insider trading liability on breach of fiduciary duty, and positing that the requisite fiduciary duty exists with respect to insiders and quasi-insiders but not with respect to market professionals, the prohibition protects the latter's ability to profit from new information about a firm.

When an insider trades on an impersonal secondary market, the insider takes advantage of the fact that the market maker's or specialist's bid-ask prices do not reflect the value of the inside information. Because market makers and specialists cannot distinguish insiders from non-insiders, they cannot protect themselves from being taken advantage of in this way. When trading with insiders, the market maker or specialist thus will always be on the wrong side of the transaction. If insider trading is effectively prohibited, however, the market professionals are no longer exposed to this risk.

Professional securities traders likewise profit from the fiduciary-duty based insider trading prohibition. Because professional investors are often active traders, they are highly sensitive to the transaction costs of trading in securities. Prominent among these costs is the specialist's and market-maker's bid-ask spread. If a ban on insider trading lowers the risks faced by specialists and market-makers, some portion of the resulting gains should be passed on to professional traders in the form of narrower bid-ask spreads.

Analysts and professional traders are further benefited by a prohibition on insider trading, because only insiders are likely to have systematic advantages over market professionals in the competition to be the first to act on new information. Market professionals specialize in acquiring and analyzing information. They profit by trading with less well-informed investors or by selling information to them. If insiders can freely trade on nonpublic information, however, some portion of the information's value will be impounded into the price before it is learned by market professionals, which will reduce their returns.

Circumstantial evidence for the demand-side hypothesis is provided by SEC enforcement patterns.
In the years immediately prior to *Chiarella*, enforcement proceedings often targeted market professionals. The frequency of insider trading prosecutions rose dramatically after *Chiarella* held insider
trading was unlawful only if the trader violated a
fiduciary duty owed to the party with whom he
trades. Yet, despite that increase in overall enforcement activity, there was a marked decline in the
number of cases brought against market professionals.

Identifying a private interest that benefits from
regulation, of course, does not necessarily mean
that the regulation is inconsistent with the public
interest. Specialists and market makers are critical
to both market efficiency and liquidity. If insider
trading causes them to increase the bid-ask spread
or take other precautions that reduce market efficiency and liquidity, an insider trading prohibition
may be in the public interest.

Market liquidity cannot be a complete explanation for the insider trading prohibition, however.
Indeed, it lacks both explanatory and normative
power. Market liquidity-based theories fail to take
into account the limited nature of the current prohibition. While the *post-Chiarella framework* significantly reduces the risk that market professionals
will be targeted for insider trading violations, giving
them a private interest in supporting that frame-

work, the *post-Chiarella regime* does not fully insulate market makers and specialists from trading with investors having superior information. Authorized traders, brazen misappropriators, persons trading while in possession of but not on the basis of inside information, and persons trading on their own intentions all may lawfully trade. In addition, because firms benefit from having liquid and efficient markets for their securities, we would expect to observe firms bonding against insider trading. Yet, by all accounts, firms did not do so even before Cady, *Roberts*. The empirical case for market liquidity-based theories is further undermined by the well-known observation that highly liquid and efficient stock markets exist in several countries that do not prohibit insider trading or fail to enforce the laws on the books, such as Japan and Hong Kong.

The insulation the current regime gives market professionals, along with the potential protections it provides them against at least some trading by persons with superior information, suffices to explain why market professionals would support the current prohibition. In order for the allegedly deleterious effects of insider trading on market efficiency and liquidity to provide a normative justification for the current prohibition, however, several conditions need to be satisfied. First, it must be demonstrated that insider trading actually reduces liquidity. Second, a ban of insider trading must promote (or, at least, not impede) market efficiency. As we have seen, however, the evidence on the market effects of insider trading remains inconclusive. If Marine's market efficiency claims are correct, market efficiency would be enhanced by repealing the prohibition.

The Case for Regulation

The arguments in favor of regulating insider trading can be separated into one set sounding in economic terms and a second set premised on fairness, equity, and other non-efficiency grounds. The non-economic arguments break down into two major sets: a claim that regulating insider trading is necessary to protect the mandatory disclosure system and a claim that insider trading is unfair. The economic arguments can be divided as follows: claims that insider trading injures investors; claims that insider trading injures firms; and claims relating to property rights in information.

Non-economic Argument #1: Mandatory Disclosure

Mandatory disclosure is arguably the central purpose of the federal securities laws. Both the Securities Act and the Exchange Act are based on a policy of mandating disclosure by issuers and others. The Securities Act creates a transactional disclosure regime, which is applicable only when a firm is actually selling securities. In contrast, the 1934 Exchange Act creates a periodic disclosure regime, which requires on-going, regular, disclosures.

As we have seen, neither Act requires a firm to disclose all nonpublic information relating to the firm. Instead, when premature disclosure would harm the firm's interests, the firm is generally free to refrain from disclosing such information. Even proponents of the mandatory disclosure system acknowledge that it is appropriate to strike this balance between investors' need for disclosure and management's need for secrecy.

It has been suggested that the federal insider trading prohibition is necessary to the effective working of this mandatory disclosure system.[131] The prohibition supposedly ensures "that confidentiality is not abused and utilized for the personal and secret profit of corporate managers and employees or persons associated with a bidder in a tender offer."[132] Many reputable corporate law scholars, of course, doubt whether mandatory disclosure is a sound policy.[133] If the mandatory disclosure system ought to be done away with, this line of argument collapses at the starting gate. For present purposes, however, we shall take the mandatory disclosure system as a given and limit our inquiry to whether a prohibition of insider trading is necessary to protect the mandatory disclosure system from abuse.

Insider trading seems likely to adversely affect the mandatory disclosure regime only insofar as it affects managers' incentives to manipulate the timing of disclosure. As the argument goes, a manager might delay making federally mandated disclosures

131. Roberta S. Karmel, *The Relationship Between Mandatory Disclosure and Prohibitions Against Insider Trading: Why a Property Rights Theory of Insider Trading Is Untenable*, 59 Brook. L. Rev. 149, 169–70 (1993).

132. Id. at 170–71.

133. E.g., Frank H. Easterbrook & Daniel R. Fischel, The Economic Structure Of Corporate Law 276–314 (1991); Roberta Romano, The Genius Of American Corporate Law 91–96 (1993).

in order to give herself more time in which to trade in her company's stock before the inside information is announced. As we shall see below, however, it is doubtful whether insider trading results in significant delays in corporate disclosures.

Indeed, insider trading seems more likely to create incentives for insiders to prematurely disclose information than to delay its disclosure. While premature disclosure threatens the firm's interests, that threat has little to do with the mandatory disclosure system. Instead, it is properly treated as a breach of the insider's fiduciary duty.

In any event, concern for ensuring timely disclosure cannot justify a prohibition of the breadth it currently possesses. As we have seen, the prohibition encompasses a host of actors both within and outside the firm. In contrast, only a few actors are likely to have the power to affect the timing of disclosure. A much narrower prohibition thus would suffice if this were the principal rationale for regulating insider trading. Indeed, if this were the main concern, one need not prohibit insider trading at all. Instead, one could strike at the problem much more directly by proscribing failing to disclose material information in the absence of a legitimate corporate reason for doing so.

Non-economic Argument #2: Insider Trading Is Unfair

There seems to be a widely shared view that there is something inherently sleazy about insider trading. Given the draconian penalties associated with insider trading, however, vague and poorly articulated notions of fairness surely provide an insufficient justification for the prohibition. Can we identify a standard of reference by which to demonstrate that insider trading ought to be prohibited on fairness grounds? In my judgment, we cannot.

Fairness can be defined in various ways. Most of these definitions, however, collapse into the various efficiency-based rationales for prohibiting insider trading. We might define fairness as fidelity, for example, by which I mean the notion that an agent should not cheat her principal. But this argument only has traction if insider trading is in fact a form of cheating, which in turn depends on how we assign the property right to confidential corporate information. Alternatively, we might define fairness as equality of access to information, as many courts and scholars have done, but this definition must be rejected in light of *Chiarella*'s rejection of the *Texas Gulf Sulphur* equal access standard. Finally, we might define fairness as a prohibition of injuring another. But such a definition justifies an insider trading prohibition only if investors are injured by insider trading, which seems unlikely. Accordingly, fairness concerns need not detain us further; instead, we can turn directly to the economic arguments against insider trading.

Economic Argument #1: Injury to Investors

Insider trading is said to harm investors in two principal ways. Some contend that the investor's trades are made at the "wrong price." A more sophisticated theory posits that the investor is induced to make a bad purchase or sale. Neither argument proves convincing on close examination.

An investor who trades in a security contemporaneously with insiders having access to material nonpublic information likely will allege injury in that he sold at the wrong price; i.e., a price that does not reflect the undisclosed information. If a firm's stock currently sells at $10 per share, but after disclosure of the new information will sell at $15, a shareholder who sells at the current price thus will claim a $5 loss.

The investor's claim, however, is fundamentally flawed. It is purely fortuitous that an insider was on the other side of the transaction. The gain corresponding to the shareholder's loss is reaped not just by inside traders, but by all contemporaneous purchasers whether they had access to the undisclosed information or not.[134]

134. To be sure, insider trading results in outside investors as a class reaping a smaller share of the gains from new information. William Wang, *Trading on Material Nonpublic Information on Impersonal Stock Markets: Who Is Harmed, and Who Can Sue Whom Under SEC Rule 10b–5?*, 54 S. Cal. L. Rev. 1217, (1981) (positing the "law of conservation of securities"). In *Texas Gulf Sulphur*, for example, the price of TGS's stock rose from about $18 to about $55 during the relevant time period. Assuming all of that gain can be attributed to information about the ore strike, and further assuming that TGS had 1 million shares outstanding, the total gain to be divided was about $37 million. If insiders pocketed $2 million of that gain, there will be $2 million less for outsiders to divide. This is not a strong argument for banning insider trading, however. First, it only asserts that investors as a class are less well-off by virtue of insider trading.

To be sure, the investor might not have sold if he had had the same information as the insider, but even so the rules governing insider trading are not the source of his problem. On an impersonal trading market, neither party knows the identity of the person with whom he is trading. Thus, the seller has made an independent decision to sell without knowing that the insider is buying; if the insider were not buying, the seller would still sell. It is thus the nondisclosure that causes the harm, rather than the mere fact of trading.[135]

The information asymmetry between insiders and public investors arises out of the mandatory disclo-

It cannot identify any particular investor who suffered losses as a result of the insider trading. Second, if we make the traditional assumption that the relevant supply of a given security is the universe of all securities with similar beta coefficients, any gains siphoned off by insiders with respect to a particular stock are likely to be an immaterial percentage of the gains contemporaneously earned by the class of investors as a whole. (Even in *Texas Gulf Sulphur*, trading by insiders amounted to less than 10% of the trading activity in TGS stock and, of course, a vastly smaller percentage of trading activity in the class of securities with comparable betas.) Finally, although the law of conservation of securities asserts that some portion of the gains flow to insiders rather than to outside investors, that fact standing alone is legally unremarkable. To justify a ban on insider trading, you need a basis for asserting that it is inappropriate, undesirable, or immoral for those gains to be reaped by insiders. The law of conservation of securities does not, standing alone, provide such a basis.

135. On an impersonal exchange, moreover, the precise identity of the seller is purely fortuitous and it is difficult to argue that the seller who happened to be matched with the insider has been hurt more than any other contemporaneous seller whose sale was not so matched.

sure rules allowing firms to keep some information confidential even if it is material to investor decision-making. Unless immediate disclosure of material information is to be required, a step the law has been unwilling to take, there will always be winners and losers in this situation. Irrespective of whether insiders are permitted to inside trade or not, the investor will not have the same access to information as the insider. It makes little sense to claim that the shareholder is injured when his shares are bought by an insider, but not when they are bought by an outsider without access to information. To the extent the selling shareholder is injured, his injury thus is correctly attributed to the rules allowing corporate nondisclosure of material information, not to insider trading.

Arguably, for example, the TGS shareholders who sold from November through April were not made any worse off by the insider trading that occurred during that period. Most, if not all, of these people sold for a series of random reasons unrelated to the trading activities of insiders. The only seller we should worry about is the one that consciously thought, "I'm going to sell because this worthless company never finds any ore." Even if such an investor existed, however, we have no feasible way of identifying him. Ex post, of course, all the sellers will pretend this was why they sold. If we believe Manne's argument that insider trading is an efficient means of transmitting information to the market, moreover, selling TGS shareholders actually were better off by virtue of the insider trading.

They sold at a price higher than their shares would have commanded but for the insider trading activity that led to higher prices. In short, insider trading has no "victims." What to do about the "offenders" is a distinct question analytically.

A more sophisticated argument is that the price effects of insider trading induce shareholders to make poorly advised transactions. It is doubtful whether insider trading produces the sort of price effects necessary to induce shareholders to trade, however. While derivatively informed trading can affect price, it functions slowly and sporadically. Given the inefficiency of derivatively informed trading, price or volume changes resulting from insider trading will only rarely be of sufficient magnitude to induce investors to trade.

Assuming for the sake of argument that insider trading produces noticeable price effects, however, and further assuming that some investors are misled by those effects, the inducement argument is further flawed because many transactions would have taken place regardless of the price changes resulting from insider trading. Investors who would have traded irrespective of the presence of insiders in the market benefit from insider trading because they transacted at a price closer to the correct price; i.e., the price that would prevail if the information were disclosed. In any case, it is hard to tell how the inducement argument plays out when investors are examined as a class. For any given number who decide to sell because of a price rise, for example, another group of investors may decide to defer a planned sale in anticipation of further increases.

An argument closely related to the investor injury issue is the claim that insider trading undermines investor confidence in the securities market. In the absence of a credible investor injury story, it is difficult to see why insider trading should undermine investor confidence in the integrity of the securities markets.

There is no denying that many investors are angered by insider trading. A Business Week poll, for example, found that 52% of respondents wanted insider trading to remain unlawful. In order to determine whether investor anger over insider trading undermines their confidence in the markets, however, one must first identify the source of that anger. A Harris poll found that 55% of the respondents said they would inside trade if given the opportunity. Of those who said they would not trade, 34% said they would not do so only because they would be afraid the tip was incorrect. Only 35% said they would refrain from trading because insider trading is wrong. Here lies one of the paradoxes of insider trading. Most people want insider trading to remain illegal, but most people (apparently including at least some of the former) are willing to participate if given the chance to do so on the basis of accurate information. This paradox is central to evaluating arguments based on confidence in the market. Investors that are willing to inside trade if given the opportunity obviously have no confidence in the integrity of the market in the first instance. Any anger they feel over insider trading therefore has nothing to do with a loss of confidence in the integrity of the market, but instead arises principally from envy of the insider's greater access to information.

The loss of confidence argument is further undercut by the stock market's performance since the insider trading scandals of the mid–1980s. The enormous publicity given those scandals put all investors on notice that insider trading is a common securities violation. At the same time, however, the years since the scandals have been one of the stock market's most robust periods. One can but conclude that insider trading does not seriously threaten the confidence of investors in the securities markets.

In sum, neither investor protection nor maintenance of confidence have much traction as theoretical justifications for any prohibition of insider trading. Nor do they have much explanatory power with respect to the prohibition currently on the books. An investor's rights vary widely depending on the nature of the insider trading transaction; the identity of the trader; and the source of the information. Yet, if the goal is investor protection, why should these considerations be relevant?

Recall, for example, *United States v. Carpenter*:[136] R. Foster Winans wrote the Wall Street Journal's "Heard on the Street" column, a daily report on various stocks that is said to affect the price of the stocks discussed. Journal policy expressly treated

136. *United States v. Carpenter*, 791 F.2d 1024, 1026–27 (2d Cir.1986), aff'd, 484 U.S. 19 (1987).

the column's contents prior to publication as confidential information belonging to the newspaper. Despite that rule, Winans agreed to provide several co-conspirators with prepublication information as to the timing and contents of future columns. His fellow conspirators then traded in those stocks based on the expected impact of the column on the stocks' prices, sharing the profits. In affirming their convictions, the Second Circuit anticipated *O'Hagan* by holding that Winans's breach of his fiduciary duty to the Wall Street Journal satisfied the standards laid down in *Chiarella* and *Dirks*. From either an investor protection or confidence in the market perspective, however, this outcome seems bizarre at best. For example, any duties Winans owed in this situation ran to an entity that had neither issued the securities in question nor even participated in stock market transactions. What Winans's breach of his duties to the Wall Street Journal has to do with the federal securities laws, if anything, is not self-evident.

The incongruity of the misappropriation theory becomes even more apparent when one considers that its logic suggests that the Wall Street Journal could lawfully trade on the same information used by Winans. If we are really concerned with protecting investors and maintaining their confidence in the market's integrity, the inside trader's identity ought to be irrelevant. From the investors' point of view, insider trading is a matter of concern only because they have traded with someone who used their superior access to information to profit at the investor's expense. As such, it would not appear to matter whether it is Winans or the Journal on the opposite side of the transaction. Both have greater access to the relevant information than do investors.

The logic of the misappropriation theory also suggests that Winans would not have been liable if the Wall Street Journal had authorized his trades. In that instance, the Journal would not have been deceived, as *O'Hagan* requires. Winans' trades would not have constituted an improper conversion of nonpublic information, moreover, so that the essential breach of fiduciary duty would not be present. Again, however, from an investor's perspective, it would not seem to matter whether Winans's trades were authorized or not.

Finally, conduct that should be lawful under the misappropriation theory is clearly proscribed by Rule 14e–3. A takeover bidder may not authorize others to trade on information about a pending tender offer, for example, even though such trading might aid the bidder by putting stock in friendly hands. If the acquisition is to take place by means other than a tender offer, however, neither Rule 14e–3 nor the misappropriation theory should apply. From an investor's perspective, however, the form of the acquisition seems just as irrelevant as the identity of the insider trader.

All of these anomalies, oddities, and incongruities have crept into the federal insider trading prohibition as a direct result of *Chiarella*'s imposition of a fiduciary duty requirement. None of them, however, are easily explicable from either an investor protection or a confidence in the market rationale.

Economic Argument #2: Injury to the Issuer

Unlike tangible property, information can be used by more than one person without necessarily lowering its value. If a manager who has just negotiated a major contract for his employer then trades in his employer's stock, for example, there is no reason to believe that the manager's conduct necessarily lowers the value of the contract to the employer. But while insider trading will not always harm the employer, it may do so in some circumstances. This section evaluates four significant potential injuries to the issuer associated with insider trading.

Delay. Insider trading could injure the firm if it creates incentives for managers to delay the transmission of information to superiors. Decision-making in any entity requires accurate, timely information. In large, hierarchical organizations, such as publicly traded corporations, information must pass through many levels before reaching senior managers. The more levels, the greater the probability of distortion or delay intrinsic to the system. This inefficiency can be reduced by downward delegation of decision-making authority but not eliminated. Even with only minimal delay in the upward transmission of information at every level, where the information must pass through many levels before reaching a decision-maker, the net delay may be substantial.

If a manager discovers or obtains information (either beneficial or detrimental to the firm), she may delay disclosure of that information to other managers so as to assure herself sufficient time to trade on the basis of that information before the corporation acts upon it. Even if the period of delay by any one manager is brief, the net delay produced by successive trading managers may be substantial. Unnecessary delay of this sort harms the firm in several ways. The firm must monitor the manager's conduct to ensure timely carrying out of her duties. It becomes more likely that outsiders will become aware of the information through snooping or leaks. Some outsider may even independently discover and utilize the information before the corporation acts upon it.

Although delay is a plausible source of harm to the issuer, its importance is easily exaggerated. The available empirical evidence scarcely rises above the anecdotal level, but does suggest that measurable delay attributable to insider trading is rare.[137] Given the rapidity with which securities transactions can be conducted in modern secondary trading markets, moreover, a manager need at most delay corporate action long enough for a five minute telephone conversation with her stockbroker. Delay (either in transmitting information or taking action) also often will be readily detectable by the employ-

137. Michael P. Dooley, *Enforcement of Insider Trading Restrictions*, 66 Va. L. Rev. 1, 34 (1980).

er. Finally, and perhaps most importantly, insider trading may create incentives to release information early just as often as it creates incentives to delay transmission and disclosure of information.

Interference with Corporate Plans. Trading during the planning stage of an acquisition is a classic example of how insider trading might adversely interfere with corporate plans. If managers charged with overseeing an acquisition buy shares in the target, and their trading has a significant upward effect on the price of the target's stock, the takeover will be more expensive. If significant price and volume changes are caused by their trading, that also might tip off others to the secret, interfering with the bidder's plans, as by alerting the target to the need for defensive measures.

The risk of premature disclosure poses an even more serious threat to corporate plans. The issuer often has just as much interest in when information becomes public as it does in whether the information becomes public. Suppose Target, Inc., enters into merger negotiations with a potential acquirer. Target managers who inside trade on the basis of that information will rarely need to delay corporate action in order to effect their purchases. Having made their purchases, however, the managers now have an incentive to cause disclosure of Target's plans as soon as possible. Absent leaks or other forms of derivatively informed trading, the merger will have no price effect until it is disclosed to the market, at which time there usually is a strong positive effect. Once the information is disclosed, the trading managers will be able to reap substantial profits, but until disclosure takes place, they bear a variety of firm-specific and market risks. The deal, the stock market, or both may collapse at any time. Early disclosure enables the managers to minimize those risks by selling out as soon as the price jumps in response to the announcement.

If disclosure is made too early, a variety of adverse consequences may result. If disclosure triggers competing bids, the initial bidder may withdraw from the bidding or demand protection in the form of costly lock-ups and other exclusivity provisions. Alternatively, if disclosure does not trigger competing bids, the initial bidder may conclude that it overbid and lower its offer accordingly. In addition, early disclosure brings the deal to the attention of regulators and plaintiffs' lawyers earlier than necessary.

An even worse case scenario is suggested by *SEC v. Texas Gulf Sulphur Co.*[138] Recall that insiders who knew of the ore discovery traded over an extended period of time. During that period the corporation was attempting to buy up the mineral rights to the affected land. If the news had leaked prematurely, the issuer at least would have had to pay much higher fees for the mineral rights, and may well have lost some land to competitors. Given the magnitude of the strike, which eventually resulted in a 300–plus percent increase in the firm's

138. 401 F.2d 833 (2d Cir.1968), cert. denied, 394 U.S. 976 (1969).

market price, the harm that would have resulted from premature disclosure was immense.

Although insider trading probably only rarely causes the firm to lose opportunities, it may create incentives for management to alter firm plans in less drastic ways to increase the likelihood and magnitude of trading profits. For example, trading managers can accelerate receipt of revenue, change depreciation strategy, or alter dividend payments in an attempt to affect share prices and insider returns. Alternatively, the insiders might structure corporate transactions to increase the opportunity for secret-keeping. Both types of decisions may adversely affect the firm and its shareholders. Moreover, this incentive may result in allocative inefficiency by encouraging overinvestment in those industries or activities that generate opportunities for insider trading.

Judge Frank Easterbrook has identified a related perverse incentive created by insider trading.[139] Managers may elect to follow policies that increase fluctuations in the price of the firm's stock. They may select riskier projects than the shareholders would prefer, because, if the risks pay off, they can capture a portion of the gains in insider trading and, if the project flops, the shareholders bear the loss. In contrast, Professors Carlton and Fischel assert that Easterbrook overstates the incentive to

139. Frank H. Easterbrook, *Insider Trading, Secret Agents, Evidentiary Privileges, and the Production of Information*, 1981 Sup. Ct. Rev. 309 (1981).

choose high-risk projects.[140] Because managers must work in teams, the ability of one or a few managers to select high-risk projects is severely constrained through monitoring by colleagues. Cooperation by enough managers to pursue such projects to the firm's detriment is unlikely because a lone whistle-blower is likely to gain more by exposing others than he will by colluding with them. Further, Carlton and Fischel argue managers have strong incentives to maximize the value of their services to the firm. Therefore they are unlikely to risk lowering that value for short-term gain by adopting policies detrimental to long-term firm profitability. Finally, Carlton and Fischel alternatively argue that even if insider trading creates incentives for management to choose high-risk projects, these incentives are not necessarily harmful. Such incentives would act as a counterweight to the inherent risk aversion that otherwise encourages managers to select lower risk projects than shareholders would prefer. Allowing insider trading may encourage management to se-lect negative net present value investments, howev-er, not only because shareholders bear the full risk of failure, but also because failure presents manage-ment with an opportunity for profit through short-selling. As a result, shareholders might prefer other incentive schemes.

Injury to Reputation. It has been said that insider trading by corporate managers may cast a cloud on the corporation's name, injure stockholder

140. Dennis W. Carlton and Daniel R. Fischel, *The Regula-tion of Insider Trading*, 35 Stan. L. Rev. 857 (1983).

relations and undermine public regard for the corporation's securities.[141] Reputational injury of this sort could translate into a direct financial injury, by raising the firm's cost of capital, if investors demand a premium (by paying less) when buying stock in a firm whose managers inside trade. Because shareholder injury is a critical underlying premise of the reputational injury story, however, this argument would appear to collapse at the starting gate. As we have seen, it is very hard to create a plausible shareholder injury story.

Economic Argument #3: A Property Rights Analysis

There are essentially two ways of creating property rights in information: allow the owner to enter into transactions without disclosing the information or prohibit others from using the information. In effect, the federal insider trading prohibition vests a property right of the latter type in the party to whom the insider trader owes a fiduciary duty to refrain from self-dealing in confidential information. To be sure, at first blush, the insider trading prohibition admittedly does not look very much like most property rights. Enforcement of the insider trading prohibition admittedly differs rather dramatically from enforcement of, say, trespassing laws. The existence of property rights in a variety of intangibles, including information, however, is well-

141. Compare *Diamond v. Oreamuno*, 248 N.E.2d 910, 912 (N.Y. 1969) (discussing threat of reputational injury) with *Freeman v. Decio*, 584 F.2d 186, 194 (7th Cir.1978) (arguing that injury to reputation is speculative).

established. Trademarks, copyrights, and patents are but a few of the better known examples of this phenomenon. There are striking doctrinal parallels, moreover, between insider trading and these other types of property rights in information. Using another's trade secret, for example, is actionable only if taking the trade secret involved a breach of fiduciary duty, misrepresentation, or theft. This was an apt summary of the law of insider trading after the Supreme Court's decisions in *Chiarella* and *Dirks* (although it is unclear whether liability for theft in the absence of a breach of fiduciary duty survives *O'Hagan*).

In context, moreover, even the insider trading prohibition's enforcement mechanisms are not inconsistent with a property rights analysis. Where public policy argues for giving someone a property right, but the costs of enforcing such a right would be excessive, the state often uses its regulatory powers as a substitute for creating private property rights. Insider trading poses just such a situation. Private enforcement of the insider trading laws is rare and usually parasitic on public enforcement proceedings. Indeed, the very nature of insider trading arguably makes public regulation essential precisely because private enforcement is almost impossible. The insider trading prohibition's regulatory nature thus need not preclude a property rights-based analysis.

The rationale for prohibiting insider trading is the same as that for prohibiting patent infringement or theft of trade secrets: protecting the eco-

nomic incentive to produce socially valuable information. As the theory goes, the readily appropriable
nature of information makes it difficult for the
developer of a new idea to recoup the sunk costs
incurred to develop it. If an inventor develops a
better mousetrap, for example, he cannot profit on
that invention without selling mousetraps and
thereby making the new design available to potential competitors. Assuming both the inventor and
his competitors incur roughly equivalent marginal
costs to produce and market the trap, the competitors will be able to set a market price at which the
inventor likely will be unable to earn a return on
his sunk costs. Ex post, the rational inventor should
ignore his sunk costs and go on producing the
improved mousetrap. Ex ante, however, the inventor will anticipate that he will be unable to generate
positive returns on his up-front costs and therefore
will be deterred from developing socially valuable
information. Accordingly, society provides incentives for inventive activity by using the patent system to give inventors a property right in new ideas.
By preventing competitors from appropriating the
idea, the patent allows the inventor to charge mo-
nopolistic prices for the improved mousetrap, thereby recouping his sunk costs. Trademark, copyright,
and trade secret law all are justified on similar
grounds.

This argument does not provide as compelling a
justification for the insider trading prohibition as it
does for the patent system. A property right in
information should be created when necessary to

prevent conduct by which someone other than the developer of socially valuable information appropriates its value before the developer can recoup his sunk costs. As we have seen, however, insider trading often has no effect on an idea's value to the corporation and probably never entirely eliminates its value. Legalizing insider trading thus would have a much smaller impact on the corporation's incentive to develop new information than would, say, legalizing patent infringement.

The property rights approach nevertheless has considerable power. Consider the prototypical insider trading transaction, in which an insider trades in his employer's stock on the basis of information learned solely because of his position with the firm. There is no avoiding the necessity of assigning a property interest in the information to either the corporation or the insider. A rule allowing insider trading assigns a property interest to the insider, while a rule prohibiting insider trading assigns it to the corporation.

From the corporation's perspective, we have seen that legalizing insider trading would have a relatively small effect on the firm's incentives to develop new information. In some cases, however, insider trading will harm the corporation's interests and thus adversely affect its incentives in this regard. This argues for assigning the property right to the corporation, rather than the insider.

That argument is buttressed by the observation that creation of a property right with respect to a particular asset typically is not dependent upon there being a measurable loss of value resulting from the asset's use by someone else. Indeed, creation of a property right is appropriate even if any loss in value is entirely subjective, both because subjective valuations are difficult to measure for purposes of awarding damages and because the possible loss of subjective values presumably would affect the corporation's incentives to cause its agents to develop new information. As with other property rights, the law therefore should simply assume (although the assumption will sometimes be wrong) that assigning the property right to agent-produced information to the firm maximizes the social incentives for the production of valuable new information.

Because the relative rarity of cases in which harm occurs to the corporation weakens the argument for assigning it the property right, however, the critical issue may be whether one can justify assigning the property right to the insider. On close examination, the argument for assigning the property right to the insider is considerably weaker than the argument for assigning it to the corporation. The only plausible justification for doing so is the argument that legalized insider trading would be an appropriate compensation scheme. In other words, society might allow insiders to inside trade in order to give them greater incentives to develop new information. As we have seen, however, this argument appears to founder because, *inter alia*, insider trading is an inefficient compensation scheme. The economic theory of property rights in information thus cannot justify assigning the property right to insiders rather than to the corporation. Because there is no avoiding the necessity of assigning the property right to the information in question to one of the relevant parties, the argument for assigning it to the corporation therefore should prevail.[142]

Implication #1: Scope of the Prohibition. In *Diamond v. Oreamuno*,[143] the New York Court of Appeals concluded that a shareholder could properly bring a derivative action against corporate officers who had traded in the corporation's stock. The court explicitly relied on a property rights-based justification for its holding: "The primary concern, in a case such as this, is not to determine whether the corporation has been damaged, but to decide, as between the corporation and the defendants, who has a higher claim to the proceeds derived from exploitation of the information." Critics of *Diamond* have frequently pointed out that the corporation could not have used the information at issue in that case for its own profit. The defendants had sold shares on the basis of inside information about a substantial decline in the firm's earnings. Once released, the information caused the corporation's stock price to decline precipitously. The information was thus a historical accounting fact of no value to

142. The argument in favor of assigning the property right to the corporation becomes even stronger when we move outside the prototypical situation to cases covered by the misappropriation theory. It is hard to imagine a plausible justification for assigning the property right to those who steal information.

143. 248 N.E.2d 910 (N.Y. 1969).

the corporation. The only possible use to which the corporation could have put this information was by trading in its own stock, which it could not have done without violating the antifraud rules of the federal securities laws.

The *Diamond* case thus rests on an implicit assumption that, as between the firm and its agents, all confidential information about the firm is an asset of the corporation. Critics of *Diamond* contend that this assumption puts the cart before the horse: the proper question is to ask whether the insider's use of the information posed a substantial threat of harm to the corporation. Only if that question is answered in the affirmative should the information be deemed an asset of the corporation.[144]

Proponents of a more expansive prohibition might respond to this argument in two ways. First, they might reiterate that, as between the firm and its agents, there is no basis for assigning the property right to the agent. Second, they might focus on the secondary and tertiary costs of a prohibition that encompassed only information whose use posed a significant threat of harm to the corporation. A regime premised on actual proof of injury to the corporation would be expensive to enforce, would provide little certainty or predictability for those who trade, and might provide agents with perverse incentives.

144. See, e.g., *Freeman v. Decio*, 584 F.2d 186, 192–94 (7th Cir.1978).

Implication #2: Federal v. State Regulation.
Even among those who agree that insider trading
should be regulated on property rights grounds,
there is no agreement as to how insider trading
should be regulated. Some scholars favor leaving
insider trading to state corporate law, just as is
done with every other duty of loyalty violation, and,
accordingly, divesting the SEC of any regulatory
involvement. Others draw a distinction between
SEC monitoring of insider trading and a federal
prohibition of insider trading. They contend that
the SEC should monitor insider trading, but refer
detected cases to the affected corporation for private prosecution. A third set favors a federal prohibition enforced by the SEC.

This debate is a wide-ranging one, encompassing
questions of economics, politics, and federalism. The
analysis here focuses on the question of whether the
SEC has a comparative advantage vis-a-vis private
actors in enforcing insider trading restrictions. If
so, society arguably ought to let the SEC carry the
regulatory load.

That the SEC has such a comparative advantage
is fairly easy to demonstrate. Virtually all private
party insider trading lawsuits are parasitic on SEC
enforcement efforts, which is to say that the private
party suit was brought only after the SEC's proceeding became publicly known. This condition
holds because the police powers available to the
SEC, but not to private parties, are essential to
detecting insider trading. Informants, computer
monitoring of stock transactions, and reporting of

unusual activity by self-regulatory organizations and/or market professionals are the usual ways in which insider trading cases come to light. As a practical matter, these techniques are available only to public law enforcement agencies. In particular, they are most readily available to the SEC.

Unlike private parties, who cannot compel discovery until a non-frivolous case has been filed, the SEC can impound trading records and compel testimony simply because its suspicions are aroused. As the agency charged with regulating broker-dealers and self-regulatory organizations, the SEC also is uniquely positioned to extract cooperation from securities professionals in conducting investigations. Finally, the SEC is statutorily authorized to pay bounties to informants, which is particularly important in light of the key role informants played in breaking most of the big insider trading cases of the 1980s.

Internationalization of the securities markets is yet another reason for believing the SEC has a comparative advantage in detecting and prosecuting insider trading. Sophisticated insider trading schemes often make use of off-shore entities or even off-shore markets. The difficulties inherent in extraterritorial investigations and litigation, especially in countries with strong bank secrecy laws, probably would preclude private parties from dealing effectively with insider trading involving off-shore activities. In contrast, the SEC has developed memoranda of understanding with a number of key foreign nations, which provide for reciprocal assistance in prosecuting insider trading and other securities law violations. The SEC's ability to investigate international insider trading cases was further enhanced by the 1988 act, which included provisions designed to encourage foreign governments to cooperate with SEC investigations.

In any event, although this debate has considerable theoretical interest, it is essentially mooted by the public choice arguments recounted above. There is no constituency that would support repealing the federal insider trading prohibition, while proposals to do so would meet strong opposition from the SEC and its securities industry constituencies that benefit from the current prohibition. The federal insider trading prohibition is doubtless here to stay.

CHAPTER 5

SECTION 16(b)

In addition to the complicated insider trading rules under § 10(b), Congress has also provided a much simpler prophylactic rule under Securities Exchange Act § 16(b). In brief, § 16(b) holds that any profits an insider earns on purchases and sales that occur within six months of each other must be forfeited to the corporation.[145] As with all prophy-

145. Section 16(b) provides:

For the purpose of preventing the unfair use of information which may have been obtained by such beneficial owner, director, or officer by reason of his relationship to the issuer, any profit realized by him from any purchase and sale, or any sale and purchase, of any equity security of such issuer (other than an exempted security) within any period of less than six months, unless such security was acquired in good faith in connection with a debt previously contracted, shall inure to and be recoverable by the issuer, irrespective of any intention on the part of such beneficial owner, director, or officer in entering into such transaction of holding the security purchased or of not repurchasing the security sold for a period exceeding six months. Suit to recover such profit may be instituted at law or in equity in any court of competent jurisdiction by the issuer, or by the owner of any security of the issuer in the name and in behalf of the issuer if the issuer shall fail or refuse to bring such suit within sixty days after request or shall fail diligently to prosecute the same thereafter; but no such suit shall be brought more than two years after the date such profit was realized. This subsection shall not be construed to cover any transaction where such beneficial own-

174

lactic rules, § 16(b) is both over-and under-inclusive. It captures all sorts of trades unaffected by the use of inside information, while missing many trades flagrantly based on nonpublic information.

Section 16(a) requires insiders to report monthly any transactions in their company's equity securities. Under § 16(b), any profits earned on purchases and sales within a six month period must be disgorged to the issuer. Shareholders of the issuer may sue insiders derivatively and a shareholder's lawyer can get a contingent fee out of any recovery or settlement.

Unlike Rule 10b–5, § 16(b) applies only to officers, directors, or shareholders who own more than 10% of the company's stock. It also applies only to insider transactions in their own company's stock. There is no tipping liability, no misappropriation liability, and no constructive insider doctrine.

There are two other important limitations on § 16(b)'s scope. First, it applies only to firms that must register under the Securities Exchange Act. Second, it applies only to stocks and convertible debt. In both respects, it is narrower than under Rule 10b–5.

Although there must be both a sale and a purchase within six months of each other in order to

er was not such both at the time of the purchase and sale, or the sale and purchase, of the security involved, or any transaction or transactions which the Commission by rules and regulations may exempt as not comprehended within the purpose of this sub-section.

trigger § 16(b), it applies whether the sale follows the purchase or vice versa. Accordingly, shares are fungible for § 16(b) purposes. The trader thus need not earn his or her gains from buying and selling specific shares of stock. Instead, if the trader unloads 10 shares of stock and buys back 10 different shares of stock in the same company at a cheaper price, he or she is liable.

Examples: (1) Susan is chief financial officer of Acme, Inc. She buys 1,000 Acme shares at $8 on February 1. She sells 1,000 shares at $10 on May 1. Because the sale and purchase took place within six months, § 16(b) is triggered. She has earned a $2 profit per share and therefore must disgorge $2,000 to Acme.

(2) Sam is senior vice president of Ajax, Inc. He has owned 10,000 shares for many years. On June 1 he sells 1,000 shares at $10. On September 15 he buys 1,000 shares at $8. He also must disgorge $2,000 to Ajax ($2 per share times 1000 shares).

Courts interpret the statute to maximize the amount the company recovers. Again, an example will be helpful:

Example: Shania is president of Acme, Inc. Her transactions were as follows:

- March 1: bought 100 shares at $10
- April 1: sold 70 shares at $12
- May 1: bought 50 shares on May 1 at $9
- May 15: sold 25 shares at $13
- December 31: sold 35 shares at $20

The December 31 sale cannot be matched with either the March 1 or May 1 purchase, because they are more than six months apart. The other transactions are all matchable. A court will match them in the way that maximizes Acme's recovery:

- Match the 25 shares sold on May 15 with 25 of the shares bought on May 1, because they have the largest price differential. With a $4 profit per share ($13 minus $9) times 25 shares, Shania owes Acme $100.

- Next match 25 of the shares sold on April 1 with the remaining 25 shares purchased on May 1 for a profit of $75 ($3 per share ($12 minus $9) times 25 shares).

- Now match the remaining 45 shares sold on April 1 with 45 of the shares bought on March 1 for a profit of $90 ($2 per share ($12 minus $10) times 45 shares).

- Shania therefore owes Acme a total of $265.

Form almost always triumphs over substance in § 16(b) cases. There are some exceptions, however, the most notable of which is the unconventional transaction doctrine. The Exchange Act defines "sale" very broadly: it includes every disposition of a security for value. For purposes of § 16(b), however, certain transactions are not deemed sales; namely, so-called unconventional transactions.

The leading case in this area is *Kern County Land Co. v. Occidental Petroleum Corp.*[146] In 1967, Occidental launched a tender offer for 500,000 shares of Kern County Land Co. (Old Kern). The offer later was extended and the number of shares being sought was increased. When the offer closed in June, Occidental owned more than 10% of Old Kern's stock. To avoid being taken over by Occidental, Old Kern negotiated a defensive merger with Tenneco. Under the merger agreement, Old Kern stock would be exchanged for Tenneco stock. In order to avoid becoming a minority shareholder in Tenneco, Occidental sold to a Tenneco subsidiary an option to purchase the Tenneco shares Occidental would acquire in the merger, which could not be exercised until the § 16(b) six month period had elapsed. Tenneco and Old Kern merged during the six month period following Occidental's tender offer. Somewhat later, more than 6 months after the tender offer, Occidental sold Tenneco stock pursuant to the option.

The successor corporation to Old Kern (New Kern) sued under § 16(b). It offered two theories. First, the merger and resulting exchange of Old Kern for Tenneco stock constituted a sale, which had occurred less than six months after the purchase effected by the tender offer. Second, the tender offer constituted a purchase and that the grant

146.   411 U.S. 582 (1973).

of the option (rather than the exercise of the option) constituted a sale. Because the option was granted less than six months after the tender offer, New Kern argued that Occidental was liable for any profit earned on the shares covered by the option. The Supreme Court rejected both of New Kern's arguments, holding that Occidental had no § 16(b) liability. Both the merger and the grant of the option were unconventional transactions and, as such, were not deemed a sale for § 16(b) purposes.

Court have identified three factors to be considered in deciding whether a transaction is conventional or unconventional: (1) whether the transaction is volitional; (2) whether the transaction is one over which the beneficial owner has any influence; and (3) whether the beneficial owner had access to confidential information about the transaction or the issuer. In the case at bar, Occidental as a hostile bidder had no access to confidential information about Old Kern or Tenneco. In addition, as to the merger, the exchange was involuntary—as the merger had been approved by the other shareholders, Occidental had no option but to exchange its shares.

In closing, a word should be said about the differing treatment of officers and directors on the one hand and shareholders on the other. An officer or director has § 16(b) liability if he is an officer or director at either the time of the purchase or the sale. In contrast, a shareholder has § 16(b) liability only if she owned more than 10 percent of the company's shares both at the time of the purchase and of the sale. In *Reliance Electric Co. v. Emerson Electric Co.*,[147] Emerson bought 13.2 percent of Dodge Manufacturing Co. stock in a hostile tender offer. To avoid being taken over by Emerson, Dodge agreed to merge with Reliance. Emerson gave up the fight and decided to sell its Dodge shares. In an attempt to minimize any potential § 16(b) liability, Emerson first sold Dodge shares representing 3.24 percent of the outstanding common stock. It then sold the remainder, which represented 9.96 percent of the outstanding. When Reliance sued under § 16(b), the Supreme Court held that shareholders are subject to the statute only if they own more than 10 percent of the stock immediately before the sale. Emerson therefore had no liability with respect to its sale of the final 9.96 percent. *Reliance* is a good example of how form prevails over substance in § 16(b)—even though Emerson's two sales were part of a related series of transactions effected pursuant to a single plan, which plausibly could have been deemed a step transaction, the court treated the second sale as having independent legal significance.

Notice that Emerson did not raise, and the Supreme Court thus did not address, the significance of the fact that Emerson had not been a 10 percent shareholder at the time it made its initial tender offer. Instead, that issue came up in *Foremost-McKesson, Inc. v. Provident Securities Co.*,[148] in which the Supreme Court held that a purchase by

147.   404 U.S. 418 (1972).

148.   423 U.S. 232 (1976).

which a shareholder crosses the 10% threshold cannot be matched with subsequent sales for § 16(b) purposes. Again, an example may be helpful.

Example: Selena is not an officer or director of Ajax, Inc. At all relevant times, Ajax has 1,000 shares outstanding. Selena's transactions are as follows:

- January 1: buys 50 shares at $10
- February 1: buys 55 shares at $10
- April 1: buys 50 shares at $10.
- May 1: sells 60 shares at $15
- May 2: sells 55 shares at $20

The January 1 purchase cannot be matched with either sale, because on January 1 Selena was not yet a 10 percent shareholder. The February 1 purchase cannot be matched with either sale because it is the transaction by which Selena became a (more than) 10 percent shareholder. Only the April 1 purchase is potentially matchable, because only at the time of that purchase did Selena own more than 10 percent of Ajax's stock. As to the sales, only the May 1 sale can be matched with the April 1 purchase. On May 2, Selena owned less than 10 percent of Ajax's stock. If Selena had been an officer or director on any one of the relevant dates, of course, all of the transactions would have been subject to § 16(b).

*

Table of Cases

References are to Pages

---

*

Index

References Are to Pages

187

STATUTORY INTERPRETATION 39, 106

SUPREME COURT 9, 49

TAKEOVERS AND INSIDER TRADING 50

TENDER OFFERS
See Rule 14e–3

TIPPING 41, 53

THEORETICAL JUSTIFICATIONS OF PROHIBITION
See Policy Debate

THEORIES OF LIABILITY
See Disclose or Abstain Rule, Equal Access Test Misappropriation Theory, Rule 14e–3, Section 16(b), and State Corporate Law